Table of Cont

FREE GIFT!

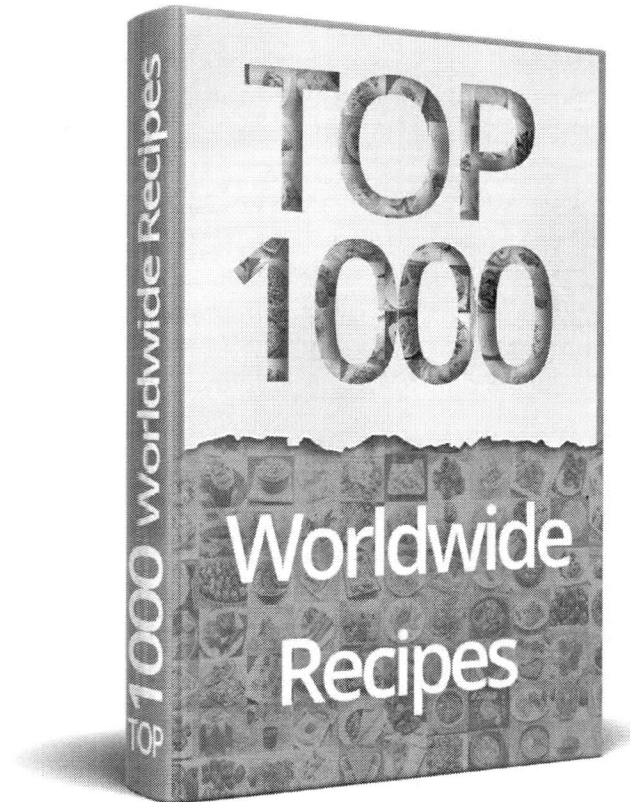

In order to thank you for buying my book I am glad to present you
- 1000 Worldwide Recipes –

Please follow this link to get instant access to your Free Cookbook: **http://booknation.top/**

Introduction

Air fryer is the new and unique invention that can help not only cook fast but also will make every your dish tasty and healthy. Air fryer is on the top of the healthiest tools for cooking. This is the indispensable cooking machine that is useful not only for chefs but also for freshmen in the cooking. The principle of work of the air machine is that the dish is cooked with the help of the hot air. Nowadays it is the healthiest way of preparing food. There are many positive sides of the air fryer. Let's consider some of them.

Firstly, it is possible to cook the dish without oil or any other fat. Such condition is important for those who follow the healthy way of life and keep fit.

The people with the allergy can be sure that the dish that was made in air fryer is safe for them. The food can be cooked fast in this miracle machine. One more good side of the tool is that the vegetables save all beneficial vitamins and microelements. The short time of preparation is the best for people who have no time for long preparation. Also, it is good for vegetables and fruits that lose the nutrients after a long heat treatment.

We described the positive features of the tool. So let's try to find the bad sides of this cooking machine. After long researching, it is possible to say that Air fryer does not have any negative feature. The one thing that is important to note that all products have their specialties that do not depend on the way of cooking. That is why it is recommended to be careful with the food you chose for your diet.

The sciences have already proved that Air fryer does not have dangerous components that can damage the human health.

The Air Fryer is good opportunity to make your favorite dish in the fast and easy way. Everything you need is an inspiration and desire to create delicious meals – all another will be done by this kitchen tool.

Breakfast recipes

Nutritional egg breakfast

It is the easiest way to be full in the morning. Add the sliced tomatoes before serving the dish.

Prep time: 10 minutes
Cooking time: 10 minutes
Servings: 3

Ingredients:
- 3 eggs
- ½ cup bacon
- 1 teaspoon butter
- 1 teaspoon salt
- ½ teaspoon paprika
- 1 onion
- 1 teaspoon fresh basil, chopped
- 1 tablespoon grated Parmesan cheese

Directions:
1. Take the mixing bowl and beat eggs in the bowl.
2. Peel the onion and chop it.
3. Combine the chopped onion and eggs together and stir the mixture gently not to destroy the eggs.
4. After this, sprinkle the mixture with salt and paprika.
5. Melt the butter and transfer it to the air fryer basket.
6. Then pour the egg mixture into the air fryer and add bacon, close the lid.
7. Cook it for 10 minutes. Then remove the eggs from the air fryer and sprinkle the dish with the chopped basil and Parmesan cheese and serve it immediately.

Sweet milk quinoa

Add honey before serving the dish – it will enforce the taste and smell of the quinoa.

Prep time: 10 minutes
Cooking time: 20 minutes
Servings: 3

Ingredients:
- 2 cup quinoa
- 1 tablespoon brown sugar
- 1 /2 cup dried fruits
- 1/3 teaspoon salt
- 1 teaspoon vanilla sugar
- 1 teaspoon maple syrup
- 4 cups milk

Directions:
1. Take the quinoa and transfer it to the mixing bowl.
2. Pour it into the 2 cups of milk and sprinkle with salt.
3. Stir the mixture carefully till salt is dissolved.
4. Then add brown sugar and the vanilla sugar. Stir it carefully again.
5. Chop the dried fruits into the tiny pieces and add them to the quinoa mixture.
6. Open the air fryer lid and transfer the quinoa mass.
7. Add maple sugar and stir the mass carefully with the help of the wooden spoon.
8. Close the lid and cook the dish for 20 minutes or till it absorbs all water.
9. Then remove the quinoa from the air fryer and let it cool briefly.
10. Serve it immediately.

Parsley muffins

The muffins are soft and fluffy. If you add your favorite spices – the taste will be delightful!

Prep time: 10 minutes
Cooking time: 10 minutes
Servings: 3

Ingredients:
- 1 egg
- 1 cup parsley
- 1 cup flour
- 1/3 cup cream
- 1 teaspoon salt
- ½ teaspoon baking soda
- 1 teaspoon lemon juice
- ½ teaspoon olive oil

Directions:

1. Take the mixing bowl and beat the egg in the bowl. Add salt and baking soda and whisk the mixture very carefully till you get homogenous mass.
2. After this, add lemon juice and olive oil. Stir it.
3. Then sift the flour into the mixture and add cream.
4. Wash the parsley carefully and chop it into the small pieces.
5. Add the chopped parsley to the flour mixture and stir it carefully till you get homogenous mass.
6. Take the muffin form and fill the ½ of every form with the muffin dough.
7. Transfer the muffins in the air fryer and close the lid.
8. Cook the dish for 10 minutes.
9. Then remove the muffins from the air fryer and let them chill.
10. Serve it.

Chicken rissole

The rissoles are light and appropriate even if you follow the diet. Add chopped dill to make the rissoles juicier.

Prep time: 10 minutes
Cooking time: 10 minutes
Servings: 3

Ingredients:
- 1 teaspoon starch
- 1 tablespoon bread crumbs
- 1 egg
- 1 garlic clove
- 10 oz minced chicken fillet
- 1 teaspoon salt
- 1 teaspoon ginger
- 1 t/2 teaspoon nutmeg

Directions:

1. Take the mixing bowl and combine the starch, salt, ginger, and nutmeg together. Stir the mixture gently.
2. Beat the egg and whisk it with the help of the whisker.
3. Then add minced chicken fillet and stir the mass carefully with the help of the hands.
4. After this, peel the garlic clove and minces it. Add the minced garlic clove to the meat mixture and stir it carefully till you get homogenous mass.
5. Make the medium balls from the chicken meat mixture and sprinkle the meatballs with the bread crumbs.
6. Open the air fryer lid and transfer the rissoles in the air fryer basket. Close the lid and the rissoles for 10 minutes.
7. When the rissoles the cooked – serve them immediately.

Pancakes

These pancakes are very soft and fluffy. Serve them with the maple syrup and butter.

Prep time: 10 minutes
Cooking time: 7 minutes
Servings: 3

Ingredients:
- 1 teaspoon baking soda
- 1 teaspoon salt
- 1 tablespoon apple cider vinegar
- 1 cup flour
- 1/3 cup skim milk
- 1 teaspoon sugar

Directions:

1. Combine salt, baking soda, sugar, and apple cider vinegar in the mixing bowl and mix up the mass very carefully.
2. After thus add the skim milk and stir it carefully again.
3. Sift the flour into the skim milk mixture and start to mix the mass with the help of the mixer. When you get smooth and homogenous mass – stop to mix it.
4. If the mixture is not liquid enough – add more skim milk.
5. Take the pancake form and pour the dough in the form.
6. Open the air fryer lid and transfer the form with the pancakes in the air fryer. Close the lid.
7. Cook the dish for 7 minutes.
8. Then remove the pancakes from the air fryer and discard them from the form.
9. Serve the pancakes immediately.

Delicious dill omelet

Dill is full of vitamins. It is a great type of the breakfast in the winter. The omelet will have light green color.

Prep time: 5 minutes
Cooking time: 7 minutes
Servings: 3

Ingredients:
- 4 eggs
- ½ cup sour cream
- ½ cup dill
- 1 teaspoon salt
- 1 teaspoon ground black pepper
- 1 teaspoon nutmeg

Directions:

1. Beat the eggs in the mixing bowl whisk them carefully. And the sour cream and stir it.
2. Sprinkle the mixture with the salt, ground black pepper, and the nutmeg. Stir it again.
3. After this, chop the fill and sprinkle the mixture with the chopped dill.
4. Then open the air fryer lid and pour the omelet mass in the air fryer basket.
5. Close the lid and cook the omelet for 7 minutes.
6. Serve it hot.

Oatmeal with blueberries

The oatmeal is one of the most useful breakfasts. Add the fresh fruits in the dish – and it will be a nutritious and tasty meal.

Prep time: 10 minutes
Cooking time: 15 minutes
Servings: 4

Ingredients:
- 2 cups oatmeal
- 3 cups water
- 1 teaspoon maple syrup
- 1 tablespoon brown sugar
- 1 cup blueberry
- 1 tablespoon butter

Directions:

1. Take the mixing bowl and put the oatmeal.
2. Sprinkle it with the brown sugar and the butter. Stir it carefully.
3. Open the air fryer lid and transfer the oatmeal mixture into it.
4. Add water and stir it carefully.
5. Close the lid and cook it for 15 minutes.
6. Meanwhile, combine the blueberries with the maple syrup and stir the mixture.
7. When the oatmeal s cooked – remove it from the air fryer.
8. Sprinkle the cooked oatmeal with the blueberry mixture and stir it gently not to damage the berries.
9. Serve it immediately.

Cabbage cutlets

The cutlets are light and delicious. You can use the blender to mince the cabbage if you do not have enough time for cooking.

Prep time: 15 minutes
Cooking time: 10 minutes
Servings: 4

Ingredients:
- 13 oz cabbage
- 1 egg
- 1 teaspoon salt
- 1/3 cup oatmeal flour
- 1 teaspoon sour cream
- 1 tablespoon olive oil
- 1 teaspoon ground pepper
- 1 teaspoon starch

Directions:

1. Take the mixing bowl and beat the egg. Whisk it carefully.
2. Add the sour cream, ground pepper, and the starch and stir the mixture every carefully.
3. After this, sprinkle the mass with the oatmeal flour.
4. Take the cabbage and wash it carefully. Then grate the cabbage with the help of the grater.
5. Combine the grated cabbage and egg mixture together.
6. Use the hand mixer to make the smooth and homogenous mass. Add olive oil and salt.
7. Stir the mixture carefully with the help of the fork and make the cutlets from the mixture.
8. Transfer the cutlets in the air fryer and close the lid.
9. Cook the cutlets for 10 minutes. Then let the dish cool briefly and serve it immediately.
10. Enjoy!

Creamy buckwheat

The buckwheat tastes the most delightful with the milk. Always add honey in the cooked dish; otherwise, it will lose all the vitamins.

Prep time: 10 minutes
Cooking time: 15 minutes
Servings: 3

Ingredients:
- 2 cups buckwheat
- 2 cups water
- 1 cup cream
- 3 tablespoon brown sugar
- 1 tablespoon honey
- 1 vanilla stick
- 1 teaspoon nutmeg
- 1/3 cup cashew
- 1 tablespoon coconut

Directions:

1. Combine the buckwheat and water together. Add cream and brown sugar. Stir the mixture well.
2. Transfer the mass in the air fryer and add the vanilla stick and cream. Stir the mixture gently with the help of the wooden spoon. Sprinkle it with the coconut and cashew. Stir it again.
3. Close the lid and cook the buckwheat for 15 minutes.
4. When the dish is cooked – remove it from the air fryer and chill the buckwheat little.
5. Sprinkle it with the honey and stir it carefully till the honey is dissolved. Sprinkle the dish with the nutmeg.
6. Serve it immediately.

Cheesy bananas

It is a new way of cooking the bananas. This breakfast will be delightful for all banana lovers!

Prep time: 15 minutes
Cooking time: 5 minutes
Servings: 3

Ingredients:
- 3 bananas
- 1 cup hard cheese
- 1 tablespoon condensed milk
- 1 teaspoon butter

Directions:

1. Peel the bananas.
2. Combine the butter with the condensed milk and whisk the mixture carefully till you get smooth mass.
3. Then make the cut across every banana and fill the bananas with the condensed milk mixture.
4. Slice the hard cheese and cover the bananas in cheese.
5. Transfer the bananas in the air fryer and close the lid.
6. Cook the bananas for 5 minutes or till you get crunchy cheese.
7. When the dish is cooked –remove it from the air fryer and chill it till the room temperature.
8. Then transfer the cheesy bananas in the serving plate very carefully to not damage them.
9. Serve the dish warm.

Cottage cheese casserole

Add more eggs to the casserole to make it softer and fluffier.

Prep time: 10 minutes
Cooking time: 20 minutes
Servings: 4

Ingredients:
- 2 cup cottage cheese
- 3 eggs
- 1 teaspoon vanilla sugar
- 2 bananas
- 1 teaspoon maple syrup
- ¼ cup sugar
- ¼ cup cream
- 3 tablespoon milk
- 1/3 cup flour

Directions:

1. Transfer the cottage cheese to the mixing bowl and blend it with the help of the hand blender till you get smooth mass.
2. Then beat the eggs in the cottage cheese and continue to blend it for 1 minute more.
3. After this, sprinkle the mixture with the vanilla sugar, cream, and milk. Blend the mass for 2 minutes more.
4. Then add flour and maple syrup.
5. Peel the bananas and chop the roughly.
6. Add the chopped bananas in the casserole mass and blend it till you get smooth and homogenous mass
7. After this, transfer the mass in the air fryer form and transfer the form in the air fryer.
8. Cook it for 20 minutes.
9. Then remove the casserole from the air fryer and chill it good.
10. Cut the casserole into pieces and serve it immediately.

Potato rissoles

You can substitute the potato with the sweet potato – in this case, the will be less caloric. If you do not use the meat for the rissoles – reduce the time of cooking to 10 minutes.

Prep time: 15 minutes
Cooking time: 15 minutes
Servings: 5

Ingredients:
- 4 big potatoes
- 1 teaspoon butter
- ¼ cup flour
- 1 teaspoon salt
- 1 teaspoon starch
- ½ cup minced beef
- 1 tablespoon BBQ sauce

Directions:

1. Peel the potatoes carefully and then grate them with the help of the grater.
2. Transfer the grated potato in the mixing bowl and add flour and salt.
3. Stir the mixture carefully and add starch. Stir the mixture very carefully.
4. Melt the butter and combine it with the minced beef. Stir the mass.
5. Combine the minced meat mixture and the potato mixture together
6. Make the medium rissoles from the mixture and transfer them in the air fryer.
7. Close the lid and cook the rissoles for 15 minutes.
8. Then remove the rissoles from the air fryer and chill them little.
9. Serve the dish with the BBQ sauce immediately.

Mushroom boats

This is very tasty and nutritious dish. You can do the experiments with the filling – just add your favorite ingredients to the dish.

Prep time: 10 minutes
Cooking time: 20 minutes
Servings: 3

Ingredients:
- 1/3 cup mushrooms
- 1 teaspoon dill
- 1.4 cup cheese
- 1 tablespoon butter
- 10 oz puff pastry
- 1 egg
- 1 potato

Directions:

1. Take the puff pastry and roll it with the help of the rolling pin.
2. Then take the muffin forms and cut the puff pastry according to the size of the forms.
3. Transfer the puff pastry in the muffin forms.
4. Slice the mushrooms and chop the dill
5. Combine the sliced mushrooms and the chopped dill in the mixing bowl.
6. Add butter and egg. Stir the mixture carefully till you get homogenous mass.
7. Then peel the potato and grate it.
8. Add the grated potato in the mushroom mixture.
9. Grate the cheese.
10. Transfer the mushroom mixture in the puff pastry boards and sprinkle them with the grated cheese.
11. Then transfer the mushroom boards in the air fryer and cook them for 20 minutes.
12. Remove the mushroom boards from the air fryer and serve them hot.

Sweet rice with raisins and prunes

Use only the basmati rice for this dish – all another types of the rice are not appropriate for the dish.

Prep time: 10 minutes
Cooking time: 15 minutes
Servings: 4

Ingredients:
- 2 cup basmati rice
- 3 tablespoon brown sugar
- 1 teaspoon vanilla sugar
- 2 cup water
- 2 cup milk
- 1 teaspoon nutmeg
- ½ cup raisins
- 1/3 cup prunes
- ½ cup nuts

Directions:

1. Combine water and milk together and stir the mixture.
2. Take the rice and transfer it to the air fryer basket. Pour the milk mixture into it and stir it carefully.
3. Then sprinkle the mixture with the vanilla sugar, brown sugar, and nutmeg. Stir it carefully.
4. After this, cut the raisins into 2 parts and chop the prunes. Crush the nuts.
5. Combine the dried fruits and the crushed nuts together.
6. Add the nut's mixture in the rice mass and stir it carefully again.
7. Close the air fryer lid and cook the rice for 15 minutes. The rice should absorb all the liquid.
8. After this, remove the cooked rice from the air fryer and transfer it to the serving bowl.
9. Chill it little and serve it immediately. Add honey if desired.

Vegetarian millet

The millet is the great choice for breakfast. Add more butter in the final dish – it will make the millet creamy.

Prep time: 10 minutes
Cooking time: 15 minutes
Servings: 2

Ingredients:
- 2 cups millet
- 1 teaspoon salt
- 4 cups vegetable stock
- 1 carrot
- 1 onion
- 1 tablespoon butter
- 1 teaspoon basil

Directions:

1. Take the millet and combine it with the vegetable stock. Sprinkle the mixture with salt and stir it carefully.
2. After this, sprinkle the mixture with basil.
3. Peel the onion and carrot and chop the vegetables into the same pieces.
4. After this add the chopped vegetables in the millet mixture and stir it carefully with the help of the wooden spoon.
5. Then open the air fryer lid and transfer the millet mass.
6. Add butter and close the lid.
7. Cook the millet for 25 minutes or till all the vegetables are soft.
8. Then remove the millet from the air fryer and stir it gently.
9. Transfer the cooked dish in the serving bowls and serve it immediately.

Chicken boards with pineapple

The combination of the chicken and pineapple will amaze you. The boards are sweet and sour at the same time.

Prep time: 15 minutes
Cooking time: 20 minutes
Servings: 4

Ingredients:
- 10 oz chicken fillet, boiled
- 1 cup pineapple
- ½ cup hard cheese
- 10 oz puff pastry
- 1 teaspoon butter
- 1 teaspoon salt

Directions:

1. Roll the puff pastry with the help of the rolling pin.
2. Take the muffin forms and cut the dough according to the muffin forms.
3. Then put the puff pastry in every form.
4. Chop the chicken fillet or cut it into the strips.
5. After this, chop the pineapple into the small pieces.
6. Combine the chopped chicken fillet and pineapple together in the mixing bowl.
7. Add butter and salt.
8. Grate the hard cheese with the help of the greter.
9. Fill the muffin forms with the chicken mixture and sprinkle it with the grated cheese.
10. Take the small amount of the dough and cover every board with it.
11. Open the air fryer lid and transfer all the muffins.
12. Close the lid and cook it for 20 minutes.
13. When the chicken boards are cooked – remove the form the air fryer and discard them from the muffin forms.
14. Serve the chicken boards warm.

Apple casserole

Add cardamom and nutmeg in the casserole – it will make the final dish perfect!

Prep time: 15 minutes
Cooking time: 20 minutes
Servings: 4

Ingredients:
- 1 cup sour apples
- 1 teaspoon cinnamon
- 1 tablespoon brown sugar
- 1 cup oatmeal
- ½ cup cream
- 1 teaspoon starch
- 1 tablespoon butter
- 1/3 cup flour

Directions:

1. Take the mixing bowl and combine the oatmeal and butter together. Add starch and cream.
2. Take the mixer and mix the mixture very carefully.
3. After this, add flour and knead the dough.
4. Chop the sour apples into the medium pieces and sprinkle them with the cinnamon and brown sugar. Stir the mixture.
5. Take the casserole from.
6. Grate the ½ of all the dough.
7. Then add the ½ of the apple mixture.
8. After this, grate the second part of the dough in the form and sprinkle the dough layer with the chopped apple mixture.
9. Open the air fryer lid and transfer the casserole to the air fryer basket.
10. Close the lid and cook the dish for 20 minutes.
11. When the casserole is cooked – do not remove it from the air fryer immediately – leave it for at least 5 minutes.
12. Only after this, remove the dish from the air fryer and serve it immediately.

Fast breakfast pizza

There is nothing better than the slice of the hot cheesy pizza. This type of pizza is easy and fast to cook. You can add any of your favorite fillings.

Prep time: 10 minutes
Cooking time: 7 minutes
Servings: 2

Ingredients:
- 1 cup sour cream
- 1 cup flour
- ¼ cup sweet corn
- ½ cup boiled chicken fillet
- 1 teaspoon paprika
- 1 teaspoon salt
- 1 teaspoon basil
- 1 sweet pepper
- 1 cup Parmesan cheese
- ½ teaspoon baking soda

Directions:

1. Take the mixing bowl and combine the sour cream, flour, and the basil together.
2. Sprinkle the mass with the salt and start to mix it with the help of the mixer.
3. When you get smooth and homogenous mass – sprinkle it with the baking soda and stir the dough carefully.
4. Then pour the dough in the air fryer form.
5. Remove the seeds from the sweet pepper and chop it.
6. Sprinkle the pizza dough with the chopped sweet cheese.
7. After this, chop the chicken.
8. Sprinkle the pizza dough with the chopped chicken and sweet corn.
9. Grate Parmesan cheese with the help of the grater and sprinkle the pizza with the grated cheese.
10. Transfer the pizza in the air fryer and close the lid.
11. Cook it for 7 minutes.
12. Then remove the pizza from the air fryer and serve it immediately.

Eggs in sweet potato

Use only the sweet potato for this dish; otherwise, you will not get that special taste that is possible to get only with the sweet potato!

Prep time: 10 minutes
Cooking time: 10 minutes
Servings: 3

Ingredients:
- 3 sweet potatoes
- 3 eggs
- 1 tablespoon tomato paste
- 1 teaspoon basil
- 1 teaspoon ground black pepper
- 1 teaspoon paprika
- 8 oz bacon
- 1 teaspoon olive oil
- 3 garlic cloves
- 1 tablespoon greens

Directions:

1. Wash the sweet potatoes very carefully and cut them across into 2 parts.
2. After this, remove the meat from the vegetables and make the "boards."
3. Mince the sweet potato meat and combine it with the basil, ground black pepper, paprika and olive oil. Stir the mixture.
4. Then peel the garlic cloves and mince it. Combine the minced garlic and bacon together and stir the mixture. After this add tomato paste and stir it carefully again.
5. Chop the greens. Fill the sweet potato boards with the bacon mixture and add spicy sweet potato meat. Then beat the egg on the every board.
6. Open the air fryer lid and transfer the sweet potato boards.
   Cook the dish for 10 minutes and remove it from the air fryer. Sprinkle the dish with the chopped greens. Serve it immediately.

Breakfast easy quiche

It has never been so easy to cook the quiche. Always use the fresh and juicy vegetables for this type of the quiche.

Prep time: 10 minutes
Cooking time: 20 minutes
Servings: 4

Ingredients:
- 1/3 cup flour
- 2 eggs
- ½ cup cream
- ½ cup broccoli
- 1 onion
- 2 tomatoes
- 1 cup Cheddar cheese
- 1 tablespoon butter
- 1 teaspoon ground black pepper

Directions:

1. Take the mixing bowl and combine the flour and eggs.
2. Take the mixer and start to mix the mixture.
3. Add the cream slowly. Mix it carefully till you get smooth mass.
4. Then sprinkle the dough with the ground black pepper.
5. Wash the broccoli carefully and make the small florets from the vegetable.
6. After this, peel the onion and chop it.
7. Slice the tomato.
8. Take the big mixing bowl and combine all the vegetables together.
9. Stir it.
10. Then add the vegetable mixture in the liquid dough and stir it.
11. Take the air fryer form and pour the liquid mixture into the form.
12. Transfer the mixture in the air fryer and cook it for 20 minutes.
13. Then remove the quiche from the air fryer and chill it little.
14. Serve it.

Lunch recipes

Stuffed eggplants

It is very soft and delicious type of lunch. You can make it at home and take outside for the picnic.

Prep time: 15 minutes
Cooking time: 20 minutes
Servings: 4

Ingredients:
- 2 big eggplants
- 1 onion
- 1 cup minced pork
- 1 egg
- 1 teaspoon white pepper
- 1 teaspoon salt
- 1 tablespoon tomato paste
- 1 teaspoon mayonnaise
- ½ cup rice
- ½ cup chicken stock
- 2 tomatoes

Directions:

1. Wash the eggplants carefully and cut them across into 2 parts. Rub the eggplants with the salt and leave them for at least 5 minutes.
2. Meanwhile, take the mixing bowl and beat the egg. Whisk it gently and add minced pork. Sprinkle the mixture with the white pepper and add rice. Stir the mixture.
3. After this, take the eggplant parts and remove the meat from them. Chop it. Combine the eggplant meat with the meat mixture and stir it carefully.
4. Then fill the eggplants with the meat mass. Slice the tomatoes and cover the eggplant boards with it. Then combine the tomato paste and mayonnaise together. Stir the mixture and cover the eggplants with it.
5. Transfer the eggplants to the air fryer and close the lid. Cook the dish for 20 minutes.
6. When the eggplants are cooked – remove them from the air fryer very carefully and serves them hot.

Kale rolls

Try something new and unnatural for your lunch. These tasty kale rolls will be a great substitute to your regular lunch.

Prep time: 20 minutes
Cooking time: 25 minutes
Servings: 7

Ingredients:
- 15 oz kale
- 1 cup rice, cooked
- 2 cups chicken stock
- 1 cup minced chicken
- 1 egg
- 1 carrot
- 2 medium yellow onions
- 1 teaspoon salt
- 1 teaspoon black pepper
- 1 cup tomato juice
- 2 teaspoon sour cream

Directions:

1. Wash the kale leaves and dry them well. Take the mixing bowl and combine the cooked rice, minced chicken, and egg. Sprinkle the mixture with the black pepper and salt. Stir it.
2. Peel the carrot and grate it. Add the grated carrot to the rice mixture. After this, peel the onions and chop them. Add the chopped onion in the mixing bowl and stir the mixture again.
3. Take the kale leaves and fill them with the rice mixture. Make the rolls and transfer them in the air fryer basket. After this, take the mixing bowl and combine the sour cream, tomato juice, and chicken stock in the bowl. Stir it carefully till you get homogenous mass.
4. Then pour the liquid into the air fryer basket too and close the lid.
5. Cook the kale rolls for 25 minutes. When the kale rolls are cooked – let them cool briefly. Then remove them from the air fryer and serve the dish warm.

Thai style rice

This type of the lunch is very nutritious – so be sure you will be full of energy after eating it. The good connection of the pineapple and the rice will make you cook this dish again!

Prep time: 15 minutes
Cooking time: 20 minutes
Servings: 3

Ingredients:
- 2 cups rice
- 4 cup beef broth
- 1 tablespoon soy sauce
- 1 teaspoon sriracha
- 1 teaspoon brown sugar
- 2 garlic cloves
- 1 teaspoon fresh ginger
- 1 carrot
- 1 teaspoon salt
- 1 tablespoon lemon juice
- 1/3 cup pineapple

Directions:

1. Take the mixing bowl and combine the rice and pineapple together. Stir the mixture.
2. Take the separate bowl and combine the sriracha, soy sauce, brown sugar, and salt together. Stir the mixture and pour it in the rice. Stir it again and leave it.
3. Peel the garlic and carrot. Mince the garlic and grate the carrot.
4. Add the vegetables in the rice and stir the mixture.
5. After this, transfer the rice in the air fryer and pour the beef broth. Mix up the mass with the wooden spoon.
6. Close the lid and cook the rice for 20 minutes.
7. When the dish is cooked – remove it from the air fryer immediately.
8. Serve it in the serving bowls and use the pineapple boards for it.
9. Enjoy!

Zucchini loaf

The zucchini loaf is very soft and fluffy. You can add all your favorite greens. It can taste good as warm as cold.

Prep time: 15 minutes
Cooking time: 25 minutes
Servings: 6

Ingredients:
- 2 big zucchini
- 1 egg
- 1 cup wheat flour
- 2 egg whites
- 2 carrots
- 1 white onion
- ½ cup oatmeal
- 1 teaspoon salt
- 1 teaspoon ground pepper
- ½ cup walnuts

Directions:

1. Wash the zucchini carefully and grate them with the help of the grater.
2. Take the big mixing bowl and transfer the grated zucchini. Sprinkle the vegetable with the salt and ground pepper. Add egg whites and egg and stir the mixture with the help of the spoon.
3. Then peel the onion and the carrots and chop them into the tiny pieces. Add the chopped vegetables in the mixing bowl with the grated zucchini.
4. After this, add wheat flour and whisk the mass very carefully. Take the loaf form for air fryer and transfer the zucchini mass in the form. Crush the walnuts and sprinkle the loaf with them. Transfer the zucchini loaf in the air fryer and close the lid.
5. Cook it for 25 minutes. When it is done – remove the loaf from the air fryer and chill it little.
6. Serve it immediately.

Tuna with cheese cover

Tuna is rich in phosphorus that is so important for our body. This lunch will be useful as for children and as for the adults.

Prep time: 20 minutes
Cooking time: 30 minutes
Servings: 4

Ingredients:
- 1 big tuna
- 1 cup Parmesan cheese
- 1 onion
- ½ lemon
- 1 tablespoon fresh ginger
- 1 teaspoon nutmeg
- 2 teaspoon salt
- 1/3 cup garlic

Directions:

1. Peel the tuna and separate it into the two fillets. Rub it with salt and sprinkle with the nutmeg.
2. Then peel the garlic and mince it. Sprinkle the tuna fillet with the minced garlic.
3. Peel the onion and chop it.
4. Slice the fresh ginger.
5. Then chop the lemon and combine it with the sliced ginger. Stir the mixture.
6. After this, transfer the tuna fillet in the air fryer form and sprinkle it with the chopped onion. Then add ginger mixture.
7. Take Parmesan cheese and grate it.
8. Make the layer of the Parmesan cheese on the tuna and transfer the fish in the air fryer. Close the lid.
9. Cook the fish for 30 minutes. You will get the baked top of the dish at the end of cooking.
10. When the tuna is cooked – remove it from the air fryer and serve it immediately.

Warm prawn salad

Use the small type of the prawns for this salad. The small prawns will enforce the delicious taste of the dish.

Prep time: 20 minutes
Cooking time: 20 minutes
Servings: 6

Ingredients:
- 13 oz prawns
- ½ cup bread crumbs
- 1 avocado
- 1 cup cream
- 1 cup grated cheese
- 1 teaspoon paprika
- ½ cup tomato
- 1 tablespoon lemon juice
- 1 teaspoon salt
- 1 tablespoon brown sugar
- 2 sweet potatoes

Directions:

1. Peel the prawns and cut them into two parts. Sprinkle them with the lemon juice and stir gently.
2. Then peel the potatoes and slice them. Sprinkle the sliced potato with salt and stir it well.
3. Peel the avocado and chop it.
4. Take the air fryer form and put the layer of the sliced potato in the form.
5. Then add chopped avocado and sprinkle the avocado layer with the paprika.
6. The sprinkle the mass with the bread crumbs.
7. Slice the tomatoes and add them in the form too.
8. After this add the ½ cup of grated cheese.
9. Then add prawns and the second part of the grated cheese.
10. Take the mixing bowl and combine the brown sugar and cream together and stir the mixture well till you get homogenous mass.
11. Then pour the mass in the prawn mixture and transfer the salad in the air fryer.
12. Cook it for 20 minutes.
13. Then remove the salad from the air fryer and let it cool briefly.
14. Serve it.

Light couscous salad

Couscous tastes great even in a salad. Every dish that consists this ingredient is tasty and will make you full fast.

Prep time: 15 minutes
Cooking time: 20 minutes
Servings: 2

Ingredients:
- 1 cup couscous
- 2 red sweet peppers
- 1 red onion
- 2 teaspoon olive oil
- 2 cups chicken stock
- 1 teaspoon chili flakes
- 2 tomatoes
- 1/3 cup raisins
- 1 zucchini

Directions:

1. Take the mixing bowl and combine the couscous and olive oil together. Add the chicken stock and leave the mixture.
2. Then peel the onion and remove the seeds from the sweet pepper.
3. Chop the vegetables and sprinkle them with the chili flakes. Stir the mixture.
4. After this, chop the tomatoes and zucchini.
5. Combine all the vegetables together and stir the mass.
6. Add raisins.
7. Then transfer the couscous mixture in the air fryer and add vegetable mass.
8. Stir it gently with the help of the wooden spoon and close the lid.
9. Cook it for 20 minutes or till the couscous will absorb all water.
10. Then remove the dish from the air fryer and serve it immediately.
11. Enjoy!

Broad beans with meat sauce

If you decided to stay for lunch at home – the broad beans would be the best dish for you. You can save your time and cook the delightful dish with this recipe.

Prep time: 20 minutes
Cooking time: 30 minutes
Servings: 4

Ingredients:
- 2 cups broad beans
- 1 red onion
- 1 cup tomato juice
- ½ cup beef stock
- 10 oz minced beef
- 1 teaspoon salt
- 2 teaspoon sugar

Directions:

1. Combine the broad beans and beef stock together in the mixing bowl.
2. Add tomato juice and minced beef. Stir the mixture gently.
3. Then sprinkle it with salt and sugar and stir it carefully again.
4. Peel the onion and chop it into the tiny pieces. Add the chopped onion in the broad bean mixture and stir it again.
5. Transfer the mass in the air fryer and close the lid.
6. Cook the dish for 30 minutes.
7. When the dish is cooked – remove it from the air fryer and stir it carefully again – all the ingredients should be soft.
8. Serve it only warm – it does not taste cold.

Mushroom wraps

This dish will be great lunch if you want to stay outside. It is easy to do and can be served as cold as warm.

Prep time: 15 minutes
Cooking time: 25 minutes
Servings: 8

Ingredients:
- 10 oz puff pastry
- ½ cup mushrooms
- 2 yellow onion
- ½ teaspoon salt
- 1 teaspoon sugar
- 1 carrot
- 1 teaspoon butter
- 1 teaspoon olive oil

Directions:

1. Take the puff pastry and roll it with the help of the rolling pin.
2. Then make the small squares from the dough and spread them with the butter.
3. Peel the carrot and onions. Chop the vegetables.
4. After this, chop the mushrooms and combine all the vegetables together. Stir the mixture carefully and sprinkle it with salt.
5. Transfer the mixture into the puff pastry squares and make the raps from every square.
6. Spread every wrap with the olive oil.
7. Open the air fryer lid and transfer the mushroom wraps.
8. Close the lid and cook the dish for 25 minutes.
9. Then open the lid and leave the wraps in the air fryer for 3 minutes more.
10. After this, remove the wraps from the machine.
11. Sprinkle the dish with butter if desired and serve it.

Pork roll with the chickpea

The pork roll is very juicy and soft. You can keep it in the fridge for 7 days as a maximum.

Prep time: 20 minutes
Cooking time: 35 minutes
Servings: 4

Ingredients:
- 15 oz pork
- ½ cup chickpea, cooked
- 1 teaspoon butter
- 1/3 cup parsley
- 1 tablespoon olive oil
- 2 tablespoon tomato paste
- 1 onion

Directions:

1. Beat the meat off gently and rub it with olive oil.
2. Chop the parsley and combine it with the cooked chickpea. Stir the mixture.
3. Peel the onion and chop it.
4. Add the chopped onion in the parsley mixture and stir it.
5. Then transfer the parsley mixture on the meat and roll it.
6. Spread the meat roll with the tomato paste.
7. Open the air fryer lid and transfer the pork roll.
8. Close the lid and cook the meat for 35 minutes.
9. When the pork roll is cooked – open the air fryer lid and remove the dish from the machine very gently.
10. Slice the pork roll into the medium pieces and let it cool briefly.
11. Serve it.

Vegetable turnovers

You can use your favorite kind of dough for the turnovers. And sprinkle the cooked dish with the sesame seeds – it will make it tastier.

Prep time: 15 minutes
Cooking time: 25 minutes
Servings: 6

Ingredients:
- 17 oz puff pastry
- 2 sweet peppers
- 1 cup cabbage
- 2 boiled eggs
- 1 tablespoon tomato paste
- 1 garlic clove
- 1 teaspoon salt
- 1 teaspoon sugar
- 1 teaspoon olive oil

Directions:

1. Take the puff pastry and roll it with the help of the rolling pin.
2. Then make the small square raps from the dough and leave it.
3. Peel the eggs and chop them.
4. Then peel the garlic clove Chop the garlic and cabbage into the tiny pieces. Combine the vegetables with chopped eggs and stir the mixture.
5. Sprinkle it with salt and sugar.
6. Remove the seeds from the sweet pepper and chop it. Add the chopped sweet pepper in the vegetable mixture too.
7. Then add tomato paste and stir it carefully.
8. Make turnovers from the puff pastry and vegetable mixture and spray them with the olive oil.
9. Open the air fryer lid and transfer the turnovers.
10. Close the lid and cook the dish for 25 minutes.
11. When the dish is cooked – remove the turnovers from the air fryer and let them cool briefly.
12. Serve it.

Stuffed dates

Baked dates have a delicious taste. It is fast to cook and appropriate as a lunch even if you follow the diet.

Prep time: 10 minutes
Cooking time: 5 minutes
Servings: 2

Ingredients:
- 10 dates
- 1 cup ricotta
- 1/3 cup walnuts
- ¼ cup minced chicken, cooked
- 1 tablespoon butter
- 1 tablespoon lemon juice

Directions:

1. Remove the seeds from the dates and cut them across.
2. Take the mixing bowl and put ricotta cheese. Add minced chicken and stir the mass carefully.
3. After thus, crush the nuts and add them to the cheese mixture.
4. Add lemon juice and butter. Stir the mixture very carefully till you get smooth and homogenous mass.
5. Fill the dates with the ricotta mixture and transfer the dates in the air fryer.
6. Close the lid and cook them for 5 minutes.
7. When the dish is cooked – remove the dates from the air fryer and serve them hot.

Pasta casserole

This creamy pasta casserole is very soft and will melt in your mouth. You can take it as a lunch at your office or enjoy it at the picnic.

Prep time: 20 minutes
Cooking time: 20 minutes
Servings: 6

Ingredients:
- 1 cup pasta
- 1 cup broccoli
- 3 cups cream
- 1 tablespoon basil
- ½ cup hard cheese
- 1 teaspoon basil
- 1 teaspoon ground black pepper
- 1 teaspoon paprika
- 3 tablespoon butter

Directions:

1. Wash the broccoli carefully and make the florets.
2. Chop the florets roughly and combine them with basil, ground black pepper, and paprika. Stir the mixture.
3. Grate the cheese and combine it with the pasta. Stir the mass gently.
4. After this, transfer the broccoli mass in the air fryer and add pasta mass.
5. Stir the mixture gently and pour cream.
6. Add butter on the top of the dish and close the air fryer lid.
7. Cook the pasta casserole for 20 minutes.
8. When the dish is cooked – remove it from the air fryer and let it cool for at least 5 minutes.

Then transfer the casserole to the serving plates and serve it immediately.

Warm creamy chicken salad

If you like warm salads for lunch – you will fall in love with this recipe. The secret of this salad is that all ingredients should be soft.

Prep time: 15 minutes
Cooking time: 30 minutes
Servings: 4

Ingredients:
- 1 eggplant
- 15 oz chicken fillet
- 1 red onion
- 2 tablespoon BBQ sauce
- ½ teaspoon dill
- 1 teaspoon cream
- ½ cup chicken stock
- 3 tablespoon mayonnaise
- 1 teaspoon sour cream
- ½ cup black olives

Directions:

1. Cut the chicken fillet into the strips and sprinkle it with the dill. Stir it gently.
2. Then peel the eggplant and chop it. Combine the chopped eggplant with the chicken strips.
3. After this, peel the onion and chop it.
4. Take the separate bowl and combine the chicken stock, mayonnaise, sour cream, and the BBQ sauce together. Whisk the mass.
5. Open the air fryer and transfer the chicken mixture. Add the black olives and stir the salad gently.
6. Then add the mayonnaise mass and stir the salad very carefully till you get homogenous mass. Close the lid.
7. Cook the salad for 30 minutes.
8. When the salad is cooked – remove it from the air fryer and stir it carefully again.
9. Serve it immediately.

Red beef soup

You can serve this soup as warm as cold. The soup will be tastier if you keep it for at least 4 hours in the fridge.

Prep time: 20 minutes
Cooking time: 30 minutes
Servings: 6

Ingredients:
- 1 cup tomato juice
- 3 cups beef stock
- 4 medium potatoes
- 1 yellow onion
- 1/3 cup green peas
- 1 teaspoon ground pepper
- 1 teaspoon salt
- 2 teaspoon cream
- 10 oz beef

Directions:

1. Take the mixing bowl and combine the tomato juice and beef stock. Stir the mixture gently.
2. Then peel the onion and the potatoes and dice them.
3. After this, chop the beef roughly.
4. Take the mixing bowl and combine all the vegetables together. Stir the mixture.
5. After this, sprinkle the mixture with the green peas, ground pepper, and salt. Stir it well.
6. Open the air fryer lid and transfer the vegetable mixture. Pour the cream in the mass. Add chopped beef.
7. Then add the tomato juice mixture and stir the dish very carefully with the help of a wooden spoon.
8. Close the lid and cook the beef soup for 30 minutes.

When the soup is cooked – all the ingredients are soft. Remove the soup from the air fryer and ladle it into the serving bowls. Serve it immediately.

Fingerling potato

The rosemary makes the potato smell great, and that is why the final dish is juicy and soft. Serve the fingerling potato only hot!

Prep time: 15 minutes
Cooking time: 25 minutes
Servings: 4

Ingredients:
- 2 cups fingerling potatoes
- 1 white onion
- 1 bay leaf
- 1 cup fresh dill
- 1/3 cup cream
- 1 cup chicken stock
- 1 teaspoon salt
- 1 teaspoon cilantro
- 1 teaspoon rosemary
- 1 tablespoon olive oil

Directions:

1. Wash the fingerling potato very carefully – do not need to peel it.
2. Toss the fingerling potato in the mixing bowl and sprinkle it with the salt, cilantro, and rosemary. Leave it.
3. Meanwhile, chop the fresh dill and combine it with the olive oil. Stir the mixture.
4. Peel the onion and chop it.
5. Open the air fryer lid and transfer the fingerling potato in the air fryer basket. Add chopped dill and bay leaf.
6. Then sprinkle the mixture with the chopped onion and pour the chicken stock. Add cream and stir the dish very carefully. The liquid should cover all the surface of the potato.
7. Close the lid and cook the dish for 25 minutes. Then leave the dish for 3 minutes to rest and remove it from the air fryer.
8. Serve It hot!

Honey ribs

They are juicy and very delicious. The ribs are sweet and sour at the same time. If you try the honey ribs once – you will love this recipe forever!

Prep time: 15 minutes
Cooking time: 35 minutes
Servings: 4

Ingredients:
- 17 oz pork ribs
- 1 tablespoon honey
- 3 tablespoon soy sauce
- 1 onion
- 1 teaspoon brown sugar
- 2 tablespoon lemon juice
- 5 tablespoon BBQ sauce

Directions:

1. Take the mixing bowl and combine honey, soy sauce, and BBQ sauce. Stir the mass carefully till you get smooth and homogenous mass.
2. Then sprinkle the mixture with the brown sugar and stir the mixture again till all the ingredients are dissolved.
3. Take the pork ribs and chop the roughly.
4. Sprinkle the chopped pork ribs with the honey mass and stir it carefully with the help of the hands. Leave the mixture for 5 minutes.
5. Meanwhile, peel the onion and sprinkle it with the lemon juice. Stir the mixture.
6. Remove the pork ribs from the honey mass and combine the meat with the onion mixture. Stir it carefully.
7. Open the air fryer lid and transfer the ribs mixture in the air fryer.
8. Pour the honey mass in the ribs and close the lid. Cook the dish for 35 minutes.
9. Then open the air fryer lid and remove the pork ribs from the air fryer basket.
10. Serve the dish hot immediately.

Sweet carrot mixture

It looks like carrot casserole – but it is better. It is very soft as flun, but at the same time the mixture is delicious and can be served as warm as cold.

Prep time: 10 minutes
Cooking time: 20 minutes
Servings: 4

Ingredients:
- 5 medium carrots
- 2 tablespoon sugar
- 2 cup cottage cheese
- 1 egg
- 1 teaspoon vanilla sugar
- 1 teaspoon cinnamon
- 3 tablespoon maple syrup

Directions:

1. Wash the carrots and peel them carefully.
2. Then grate it with the help of the grater and sprinkle the grated carrot with the vanilla sugar and cinnamon.
3. Take the big mixing bowl and toss the cottage in the bowl. Blend it with the help of the hand blender till you get smooth mass.
4. Sprinkle the cottage cheese with the sugar and maple syrup. Stir it carefully and add egg.
5. Continue to blend the mass for 2 minutes more.
6. After this, add the grated carrot and stir it gently again.
7. Open the air fryer lid and transfer the cottage cheese mixture. Close the lid.
8. Cook the dish for 20 minutes. You will get the baked surface.
9. Then remove the dish from the air fryer and let it cool briefly.
10. Serve it immediately.

Delicious potato mixture

You can serve the dish as pie or cut it into pieces or serve it by portions. Never serve the dish cold - preheat it and enjoy.

Prep time: 15 minutes
Cooking time: 30 minutes
Servings: 4

Ingredients:
- 4 potatoes
- 1 cup hard cheese
- 3 tomatoes
- 2 yellow onions
- 1 green zucchini
- 1 teaspoon salt
- ¼ cup fresh parsley
- 1 teaspoon ground white pepper
- 1 teaspoon cilantro
- 1 cup chicken stock
- 8 oz ham

Directions:

1. Peel the potato and slice it. Transfer the sliced potato in the mixing bowl and sprinkle it with the salt and cilantro. Stir the mixture.
2. Dice the ham and chop the fresh parsley.
3. Wash the green zucchini carefully and chop it.
4. Peel the onions and chop them too.
5. Transfer the chopped vegetables in the potato mixture and sprinkle it with the chopped parsley and ham.
6. Wash the tomatoes and slice them. Grate the cheese.
7. Open the air fryer lid and transfer the vegetable mass in the air fryer basket.
8. Sprinkle it with salt and ground black pepper. Add sliced tomatoes.
9. Then make the layer from the grated cheese and close the lid.
10. Cook it for 30 minutes.
11. When the dish is cooked – remove it from the air fryer carefully and serve it.

Zucchini crumble

The crumble is great with every type of the vegetables. You can substitute the zucchini with carrot or add apples and make the sweet crumble.

Prep time: 15 minutes
Cooking time: 25 minutes
Servings: 4

Ingredients:
- 2 cups bread crumbs
- 3 green zucchini
- 2 eggs
- ½ cup cream
- ¼ cup flour
- 1 teaspoon white pepper
- 1 teaspoon cilantro
- 1 teaspoon sour cream
- 1 teaspoon chili pepper
- 8 oz Cheddar cheese
- 3 tomatoes
- 1 carrot

Directions:

1. Wash the green zucchini and slice them. Then transfer the sliced zucchini in the mixing bowl and sprinkle them with the white pepper and cilantro. Stir the mass.
2. After this, take the separate bowl and beat the egg. Whisk it carefully.
3. Then add sour cream, cream, and flour. Mix up the mass with the help of the hand blender.
4. Grate Cheddar cheese. Peel the carrot. Slice the carrot and tomatoes.
5. Then open the air fryer and sprinkle the air fryer basket with the 1/3 of all bread crumbs. Then make the layer from the zucchini, carrots, and tomatoes. Pour the 1/3 of the dough and sprinkle the mixture with the bread crumbs again.
6. Repeat these steps for 5 times.
7. Sprinkle the last layer with the grated cheese and close the lid.
8. Cook the crumble for 25 minutes.
9. Remove the crumble from the air fryer and chill it little. Serve it.

Side dishes

Soft air fryer cauliflower

Cauliflower is rich in vitamins and microelements that are important for us every day. This dish is easy to cook and will be a great side dish for your dinner.

Prep time: 15 minutes
Cooking time: 20 minutes
Servings: 4

Ingredients:
- 15 oz cauliflower
- 1 teaspoon salt
- 2 egg yolks
- 1 cup cream
- 1 teaspoon white pepper
- 1 teaspoon ground black pepper
- 4 tablespoon flour
- 1 teaspoon cilantro
- 1 teaspoon chili pepper
- 2 tablespoon butter

Directions:

1. Wash the cauliflower carefully and make the medium florets.
2. Then transfer the cauliflower florets in the mixing bowl and sprinkle it with salt. Stir it gently.
3. Take the separate mixing bowl and put the egg yolk. Whisk the mixture. Then add cream and continue to whisk it till it is smooth.
4. Then sprinkle the liquid with the cilantro, chili pepper, butter, white pepper, and ground black pepper. Stir it carefully.
5. Add flour and mix it up with the help of the mixer till you get homogenous mass.
6. Then dip the cauliflower florets in the yolk mixture.
7. Transfer the dipped cauliflower florets in the air fryer and close the lid.
8. Cook the dish for 20 minutes.
9. Then serve it immediately.

Garlic red apples

The dish is spicy and sweet at the same time. It has great flavor and will be an excellent choice for the side dish! It will taste the best with pork steak.

Prep time: 10 minutes
Cooking time: 15 minutes
Servings: 4

Ingredients:
- 6 red sweet apples
- ½ cup garlic clove
- 1 teaspoon salt
- 3 tablespoon honey
- 1 teaspoon ground ginger
- 1 teaspoon brown sugar
- 1 tablespoon lemon juice
- 1 teaspoon olive oil
- 1/3 teaspoon cinnamon
- 1 tablespoon fresh parsley

Directions:

1. Wash the red sweet apples very carefully and slice them into pieces.
2. Sprinkle the apples with the lemon juice.
3. Then chop the parsley and combine it with the cinnamon, olive oil, brown sugar, salt, and ground ginger. Stir the mixture every carefully.
4. After this transfer, the mixture into the sliced apples and stir it.
5. Add honey and stir it again.
6. Peel the onion and mince it.
7. Sprinkle the apple mixture with the minced onion and stir it again. Leave the mass for at least 2 minutes.
8. Open the air fryer lid and transfer the red sweet apple mixture in the basket.
9. Close the lid and cook the dish for 15 minutes. You should get soft apples at the end of the cooking.
10. When the dish is cooked – let it cool briefly and serve it immediately.

Sweet and crispy carrot sticks

This is the perfect side dish if you cook for children. The carrot is rich in carotene that is crucial for our health!

Prep time: 10 minutes
Cooking time: 20 minutes
Servings: 4

Ingredients:
- 4 medium long carrots
- 1 egg yolk
- ½ cup cream
- 1 teaspoon water
- 2 tablespoon whole wheat flour
- 1 teaspoon salt
- 1 tablespoon oregano
- 1 teaspoon butter
- 1 teaspoon stevia

Directions:

1. Wash the carrots carefully and then peel them.
2. Make the medium size sticks from the carrot and sprinkle them with the salt. Stir the mixture carefully.
3. After this, take the separate bowl and combine the whole wheat flour, oregano, butter, and stevia together. Add the egg yolk and cream and stir the mixture little.
4. Then add water.
5. Take the hand mixer and start to mix the mass up till you get smooth and homogenous mass.
6. Then dip every carrot stick in the flour mixture. Transfer the dipped carrot sticks in the air fryer basket and close the lid.
7. Cook the dish for 20 minutes or till you get a crunchy crust.
8. Then open the air fryer lid and remove the dish from the basket.
9. Let the carrot sticks chill little and serve them immediately.

Potato pancakes

You can substitute the potato with the sweet potato – doing this the side dish will have a special taste.

Prep time: 20 minutes
Cooking time: 15 minutes
Servings: 4

Ingredients:
- 4 big potatoes
- 3 garlic cloves
- 1 yellow onion
- 1 egg
- 2 tablespoon flour
- 1 teaspoon starch
- 1 teaspoon ground white pepper
- 1/3 cup fresh cilantro
- 1 teaspoon dry dill
- ½ teaspoon salt
- 1 teaspoon flax seed's oil

Directions:

1. Take the potatoes and peel them with the help of the grater. Transfer the grated potato in the mixing bowl and sprinkle it with the starch and cilantro. Then add dry dill and flex seeds. Stir the mass carefully.
2. Peel the onion and the garlic cloves and chop the vegetables into the tiny pieces. Combine the vegetables together.
3. After this, chop the fresh cilantro and combine it with the chopped onion mixture.
4. Add this mass in the grated potato mixture and stir it carefully.
5. After this, add flour and egg. Stir the mass carefully till you get smooth mass.
6. Take the air fryer tray and make the pancakes from the potato dough.
7. Transfer the air fryer tray with the potato pancakes in the air fryer and close the lid.
8. Cook the dish for 15 minutes.
9. Then remove the pancakes from the air fryer and serve them immediately.

Aromatic asparagus

This side dish has a rich flavor and tastes the best with Italian food.

Prep time: 15 minutes
Cooking time: 25 minutes
Servings: 4

Ingredients:
- 2 cups asparagus
- ½ cup cashew
- 1/3 cup raisins
- 1 cup water
- 1 teaspoon honey
- 1 teaspoon soy sauce
- 1 tablespoon cilantro
- 1 teaspoon ground red pepper
- ½ teaspoon salt

Directions:

1. Wash the asparagus and cut it into 2 parts. Then transfer the asparagus parts in the mixing bowl and sprinkle it with the cilantro and salt. Stir it gently.
2. Combine the cashew and raisins together in the mixing bowl. Add honey and soy sauce. Stir the mixture gently.
3. Then sprinkle it with the ground red pepper and stir it again.
4. Combine the asparagus and soy sauce mixture together and stir it well.
5. Open the air fryer lid and transfer the asparagus mixture.
6. Pour the water into the dish and close the lid.
7. Cook the asparagus for 25 minutes.
8. Then open the instant pot lid and remove the asparagus mixture carefully.
9. Serve it immediately.

Spicy Brussel sprouts

You have never tried something like this before. The Brussel sprouts that are made by this recipe are soft and spicy. They taste the best with the fish dishes.

Prep time: 15 minutes
Cooking time: 25 minutes
Servings: 6

Ingredients:
- 15 oz Brussel sprouts
- 1 teaspoon cardamom
- 1 teaspoon red chili pepper
- 1 teaspoon black pepper
- 1 cup Parmesan cheese
- 1teaspoon coriander
- ½ teaspoon thyme
- 1 teaspoon salt
- 2 tablespoon butter
- 1 cup chicken stock
- 1 teaspoon sriracha
- 1 white onion

Directions:

1. Wash the Brussel sprouts carefully and cut them into two pieces.
2. Transfer the Brussel sprouts in the mixing bowl and sprinkle it with the cardamom, red chili pepper, black pepper, coriander, and thyme. Then add salt and stir the mixture very carefully.
3. Peel the onion and dice it. Combine the diced onion with the sriracha and the chicken stock. Mix up the mass.
4. Grate Parmesan with the help of the grater.
5. Combine the Brussel sprout mixture and onion mixture together and stir it carefully.
6. Then open the air fryer lid and transfer the onion mixture to the air fryer basket.
7. Sprinkle the dish with the grated Parmesan cheese and stir it gently.
8. Close the lid and cook the dish for 25 minutes.
9. When the dish is done – remove it from the air fryer and do not stir it anymore.
10. Serve it immediately.

Delightful mushrooms with the sour cream

There is no better side dish for the beef than mushrooms. This dish has a great aroma and gently taste.

Prep time: 15 minutes
Cooking time: 30 minutes
Servings: 4

Ingredients:
- 3 cups mushrooms
- ½ cup milk
- 2 tablespoon butter
- 1 onion
- 1/3 cup walnuts
- ½ cup beef broth
- 1 teaspoon ginger
- 1 teaspoon turmeric
- 1 tablespoon cilantro
- 3 apricots
- 1 teaspoon sugar
- ½ teaspoon kosher salt

Directions:

1. Slice the mushrooms and sprinkle them with the ginger and cilantro. Stir the mixture. Chop the apricots roughly.
2. Peel the onion and chop it. Combine the chopped onion with the apricots and stir the mixture. After this, crush the nuts.
3. Transfer the sliced mushrooms and onion mixture in the air fryer basket. Sprinkle the mixture with the crushed nuts.
4. Then sprinkle the dish with the turmeric, sugar, and kosher salt. Stir the mixture carefully with the wooden spoon. Add butter.
5. Combine the beef broth and milk together in the mixing bowl and mix it up.
6. Pour the liquid into the air fryer basket and close the lid.
7. Cook it for 30 minutes.
8. When the dish is cooked – open the lid and remove it from the air fryer. Let it cool little. Then serve it immediately.

Honey butternut squash

You will like this side dish from the first taste. It is soft and sweet but can be excellent side dish almost for everything.

Prep time: 15 minutes
Cooking time: 20 minutes
Servings: 4

Ingredients:
- 3 cups butternut squash
- 1 teaspoon brown sugar
- 1 teaspoon stevia extract
- 1 tablespoon coriander
- ½ teaspoon turmeric
- 1 teaspoon cardamom
- 1 teaspoon sesame seeds
- 1 tablespoon flax seeds
- ½ cup water
- 1 carrot

Directions:

1. Peel the butternut squash and chop it into the medium pieces. Sprinkle it with the cardamom and stir gently.
2. Then take the mixing bowl and combine sugar, stevia extract, coriander, turmeric, sesame seeds, and the flax seeds. Stir the mixture carefully.
3. Peel the carrot and chop it into the same pieces as the butternut squash was chopped.
4. Combine the chopped carrot and the butternut squash together and stir the mixture gently.
5. After this sprinkle it with the spice mass and stir it well.
6. Transfer the mixture in the air fryer and pour water.
7. Close the lid and cook it for 20 minutes. When the dish is cooked –open the air fryer lid and stir the dish gently with the wooden spoon.
8. Transfer the dish to the serving plates and enjoy!

Sweet corn

The corn is sweet and spicy at the same time. The jalapeno pepper gives the great flavor of the side dish!

Prep time: 10 minutes
Cooking time: 20 minutes
Servings: 4

Ingredients:
- 4 cups sweet corn
- ½ cup yogurt
- 1 cup milk
- 1 teaspoon cilantro
- ½ cup hard cheese
- 1 onion
- 1 cup prawns
- 1 teaspoon salt
- ½ teaspoon ground white pepper

Directions:

1. Put the sweet corn in the mixing bowl and sprinkle it with the cilantro, Stir the mixture.
2. Then grate the hard cheese. Combine the grated cheese with the yogurt and milk and stir the mass. Add salt and stir it again till the salt is dissolved.
3. After this, peel the prawns and sprinkle them with the ground black pepper.
4. Peel the onion and chop it. Add the chopped onion in the prawn mass.
5. Then take the big mixing bowl and combine all the ingredients together. Mix the mass up till you get homogenous consistency.
6. After thus, transfer the mixture in the air fryer basket and close the lid.
7. Cook it for 20 minutes.
8. Then remove the sweet corn from the air fryer and stir it carefully again.
9. Transfer the dish to the serving plates and serve it.

Aromatic zucchini sticks

*This is one of the most useful side dishes you ever tried. Thanks to the mixture of the spices —
the vegetables have wonderful taste and smell.*

Prep time: 15 minutes
Cooking time: 15 minutes
Servings: 4

Ingredients:
- 2 zucchini
- 1 tablespoon soy sauce
- 1 teaspoon cardamom
- 1 teaspoon salt
- ½ teaspoon ground black pepper
- 1 tablespoon sunflower oil
- 1 teaspoon thyme
- 1 teaspoon cardamom
- 1 teaspoon lemon juice
- 3 tablespoon water
- 1 teaspoon red wine

Directions:

1. Take the zucchini and wash them well. Then cut every vegetable into two parts.
2. After this, make the medium strips from the zucchini and toss them in the mixing bowl.
3. Then take the separate mixing bowl and combine the salt, ground pepper, thyme, and cardamom. Stir the spice mixture gently and add red wine. Stir it carefully again till the salt is dissolved.
4. After this, add lemon juice and stir the mass gently again.
5. Pour the mass in the zucchini sticks and stir it gently with the help of the hands to not damage the vegetables.
6. Take the bowl and combine the water and lemon juice. Stir it.
7. Add the liquid to the zucchini mixture and stir it gently.
8. After this, open the air fryer lid and transfer the zucchini into the air fryer basket.
9. Spray the mixture with the sunflower oil and close the lid.
10. Cook it for 15 minutes.
11. When the zucchini is cooked — remove them from the air fryer and chill the little.
12. Serve the dish.

Delicious air fryer parsnip

Try something new for your side dish. The parsnip will be a great addition to your fish recipes.

Prep time: 15 minutes
Cooking time: 15 minutes
Servings: 4

Ingredients:
- 2 cups parsnip
- 1 tablespoon chili flakes
- 1 teaspoon sugar
- 1 teaspoon honey
- 1/2 cup water
- 1 egg
- 1 teaspoon ground black pepper
- 1 teaspoon cilantro
- ½ tablespoon olive oil

Directions:

1. Wash the parsnip carefully and peel it. Then cut the vegetable into the strips.
2. Transfer the parsnip strips in the mixing bowl and add honey. Stir the mass carefully.
3. Take the mixing bowl and beat the egg. Whisk the mixture carefully with the help of the hand whisker.
4. After this, sprinkle the whisked egg with the sugar, ground black pepper, and cilantro. Stir the mixture.
5. Add chili flakes and stir it again.
6. Then add water in the egg mass. Stir it carefully till you get smooth and homogenous mass.
7. Open the instant pot lid and pour olive oil in the air fryer basket.
8. After this, transfer the parsnip strips in the air fryer and pour the egg mixture.
9. Stir it gently with the help of the wooden spoon and close the lid.
10. Cook the dish for 15 minutes. Then remove the dish from the water and discard all the liquid.
11. Serve it.

Sweet peach side dish

The great combination of the ham and peach make this side dish aromatic and tasty.

Prep time: 15 minutes
Cooking time: 20 minutes
Servings: 4

Ingredients:
- 4 peaches
- 2 cups ham
- 1 cup Cheddar cheese
- 1 teaspoon oregano
- 1 tablespoon chopped dill
- 1/3 cup cream
- 1 onion
- 2 sweet potatoes

Directions:

1. Wash the peaches carefully and remove the ossicles from them. Chop the roughly.
2. Slice the ham and combine it with the chopped peaches.
3. Then take the cheese and grate it with the help of the grater.
4. Take the mixing bowl and combine the chopped dill and oregano. Stir it gently.
5. Add cream and stir it again.
6. Peel the sweet potatoes and onion.
7. Chop the vegetables and combine them together. Sprinkle the vegetables with the spice mixture. Add peach mixture and mix up the mass.
8. Then sprinkle the mixture with the grated cheese and stir the mixture again with the help of the fork.
9. Transfer the mixture in the air fryer and close the lid.
10. Cook the dish for 20 minutes.
11. When the dish is cooked – remove it from the air fryer and chill it little.
12. Then stir the dish carefully and serve it immediately.

Delicious pumpkin stew

This side dish will make you love pumpkin. Use the sweet type of the pumpkin to make the special final taste.

Prep time: 20 minutes
Cooking time: 15 minutes
Servings: 4

Ingredients:
- 3 cups sweet pumpkin
- 2 green zucchini
- 1 cup fresh parsley
- 2 cups chicken stock
- 1 sweet potato
- 2 red onion
- 1 teaspoon basil
- 1 teaspoon ground black pepper
- 1 teaspoon white pepper
- 1 teaspoon cilantro
- 1 tablespoon tomato paste

Directions:

1. Peel the pumpkin and chop it into the medium pieces. Sprinkle the chopped pumpkin with cilantro and white pepper. Stir the mixture.
2. Then peel the onion and sweet potato. Chop the vegetables into the same pieces as you chopped the pumpkin. Add the vegetables to the pumpkin mixture and sprinkle it with the basil and the ground black pepper. Stir it again.
3. Wash the zucchini carefully and chop it. Add the chopped zucchini in the mixing bowl with the pumpkin.
4. Add tomato paste.
5. Chop the fresh parsley and add the chopped parsley to the mixing bowl too,
6. Open the air fryer lid and transfer the mass. Pour the chicken stock and stir it gently with the help of the wooden spoon.
7. Close the lid and cook the dish for 15 minutes,
8. When the dish is cooked —remove it from the air fryer and chill it little.
   Serve it.

Sweet chickpea

This side dish tastes the best with the chicken strips and sour sauce. It tastes the best hot.

Prep time: 15 minutes
Cooking time: 30 minutes
Servings: 6

Ingredients:
- 5 cups chickpea
- 1 cup breadcrumbs
- 1 teaspoon ground black pepper
- 7 cups chicken stock
- 1 teaspoon chili flakes
- 1 tablespoon sugar
- ½ teaspoon salt
- 1 tablespoon olive oil

Directions:

1. Take the chickpea and wash it carefully.
2. Take the mixing bowl and combine the olive oil and salt together. Whisk the mass and add chili flakes.
3. Sprinkle the chickpea with the olive oil mixture and stir it very carefully.
4. Then ass sugar and the ground black pepper. Stir it again.
5. Open the air fryer lid and transfer the chickpea mixture in the air fryer.
6. Pour the chicken stock into the air fryer and close the lid.
7. Cook the dish for 30 minutes.
8. When the dish is cooked – remove it from the air fryer and discard the chickpea from the liquid.
9. Transfer the dish to the serving plate and sprinkle it with the breadcrumbs. Stir it gently and serve it.

Honey red onion petals

The onion can taste good not only as the ingredient for the main dishes – it tastes perfect with honey and spices.

Prep time: 15 minutes
Cooking time: 10 minutes
Servings: 4

Ingredients:
- 8 big red onions
- ½ cup parsley
- 1 tablespoon brown sugar
- ½ tablespoon salt
- 1 tablespoon olive oil
- 2 tablespoon water
- 1 teaspoon apple cider vinegar
- 1 teaspoon lemon juice

Directions:

1. Take the red onions and peel them.
2. Make the petals from the onion and transfer them to the mixing bowl.
3. Sprinkle the mixture with the brown sugar and salt. Stir the mixture gently.
4. Add olive oil and lemon juice. Then add apple cider vinegar and stir the mass carefully. Leave it for at least 5 minutes.
5. Chop the parsley and add the chopped parsley in the mixture. Stir it.
6. Open the air fryer lid and transfer and onion petals. Add water and stir it gently.
7. Close the lid and cook the onions for 10 minutes.
8. Then remove the onion petals from the air fryer and stir the dish little.
9. Serve it.

Lentil and chicken salad

This side dish is so delicious and easy to cook. You can substitute the chicken with any of your favorite type of meat.

Prep time: 15 minutes
Cooking time: 30 minutes
Servings: 4

Ingredients:
- 3 cups lentils
- ½ cup chicken fillet
- 6 cups chicken stock
- ½ cup fresh cilantro
- ½ cup parsley
- ½ cup bacon
- 1 teaspoon sugar
- 1 teaspoon salt
- 1 tablespoon butter
- 1 teaspoon black pepper
- 3 tablespoon cream

Directions:

1. Take the chicken fillet and cut it into the strips and transfer the meat to the mixing bowl. Sprinkle the meat with the salt and black pepper. Stir it gently and add cream. Stir it gently again. Leave the mixture for at least 5 minutes.
2. Meanwhile, chop the fresh cilantro and dill.
3. Open the air fryer lid and transfer the lentils to the air fryer basket. Add the greens mixture and stir it. After this, add the chicken stock and sugar. Chop the bacon and add it to the lentils mixture too. Stir the mass again.
4. Then add chicken strips and mix the mixture up. Close the lid. Cook the dish for 30 minutes. When it is done – remove the dish from the air fryer and stir it again. Serve it.

The lentil side dish with the rice pasta

It is an amazing combination of the Japan style salad and European lentil salad. With this dish, you will bring a new note in your everyday meal.

Prep time: 10 minutes
Cooking time: 10 minutes
Servings: 7

Ingredients:
- 2 cups rice pasta
- 4 cups lentils
- 1 cup parsnip
- 6 cups water
- 1 teaspoon soy sauce
- 1 teaspoon pineapple juice
- 1 teaspoon salt
- 2 tablespoon olive oil
- 1 teaspoon sriracha
- 1 tablespoon fish sauce
- 1 yellow onion

Directions:

1. Peel the parsnip and chop it into the tiny pieces.
2. Take the mixing bowl and combine the chopped parsnip and the lentils. Stir the mixture.
3. Combine the soy sauce and the fish sauce together in the mixing bowl. Stir the liquid and add sriracha and salt. Stir it again and add pineapple juice and olive oil. Stir it again.
4. Then peel the onion and chop it too.
5. Combine all the ingredients together and pour water in the mixture. Stir it gently.
6. Transfer the mixture in the air fryer and add rice pasta. Cook the dish for 10 minutes.
7. Then open the air fryer lid and stir the mixture again. Remove the dish from the air fryer and transfer the dish to the serving plates.
8. Serve the dish immediately

Crusty air fryer potato

You will fall in love with this side dish because it is appropriate for any main dish. The crusty surface of the potato will emphasize the soft taste of the inside part of the dish.

Prep time: 15 minutes
Cooking time: 30 minutes
Servings: 4

Ingredients:
- 1 cup granola
- 1 teaspoon butter
- 2 teaspoon olive oil
- 1 teaspoon salt
- 6 potatoes
- 1 cup minced beef
- 1 cup chopped basil
- 3 yellow onions
- 1 cup cream

Directions:

1. Peel the potato and slice it. Sprinkle the sliced potato with the salt and olive oil and stir it gently.
2. Peel the onions and chop them.
3. After this, take the air fryer form and transfer the sliced potato.
4. Transfer the minced beef in the form too.
5. Then add chopped onion and sprinkle the mass with the chopped basil.
6. Pour the cream over the mixture and sprinkle it with the granola.
7. Transfer the air fryer form in the air fryer and close the lid.
8. Cook the dish for 30 minutes.
9. When the dish is cooked – remove it from the air fryer and let it cool briefly.
10. Serve it immediately.

Rice with cottage cheese in pumpkin

The dish is perfect for your holidays or meeting with friends. You will like not only the cooking but also the serving of the dish.

Prep time: 15 minutes
Cooking time: 20 minutes
Servings: 4

Ingredients:
- 2 onions
- 1 teaspoon salt
- 2 teaspoon brown sugar
- 1 cup rice, cooked
- ½ cup spinach
- 1/3 cup cottage cheese
- 1 butternut squash
- ¼ cup sweet corn
- 1 teaspoon paprika

Directions:

1. Peel the onions and chop them into the tiny pieces.
2. Transfer the chopped onions in the mixing bowl and sprinkle them with the brown sugar. Add salt. Stir the mass very carefully.
3. Wash the butternut squash very carefully and remove the seeds from the vegetable.
4. Cut the vegetable into the 4 pieces.
5. Add the cooked rice to the mixing bowl with the chopped onion.
6. After this, add cottage and stir the mixture very carefully.
7. Sprinkle it with the sweet corn and paprika. Mix up the mass again.
8. Chop the spinach and add it to the mixture too.
9. Then fill the butternut squash parts with the rice mixture and transfer the dish in the air fryer.
10. Close the lid and cook it for 20 minutes.
11. When the dish is cooked – chill it well and serve it immediately.

Couscous with the pumpkin seeds

The side dish is soft and tender. It can be a great addition to your pork dishes.

Prep time: 15 minutes
Cooking time: 25 minutes
Servings: 4

Ingredients:
- 3 cups couscous
- 6 cups chicken stock
- 1 teaspoon salt
- 3 tablespoon butter
- ¼ cup cream
- 1 cup pumpkin seeds
- 1 cup pumpkin
- 3 sweet pepper
- 1 cup basil

Directions:

1. Transfer the couscous in the air fryer and pour the chicken stock.
2. Sprinkle the mixture with salt and add butter. Stir it gently with the help of the wooden spoon.
3. Then remove the seeds from the sweet peppers and chop them roughly.
4. Peel the pumpkin and chop it too.
5. Combine the vegetables in the mixing bowl and add the pumpkin seeds.
6. Then chop the basil and add it to the vegetable mixture too.
7. Transfer the vegetable mixture in the air fryer and stir the mass gently.
8. Close the lid and cook the dish for 25 minutes.
9. When the dish is cooked – the couscous will absorb all liquid. Stir the cooked dish carefully and serve it immediately.

Snacks and Appetizers

Chicken balls

This is the favorite snack for the children and adults. The chicken balls are very delightful and can be served as cold as hot.

Prep time: 10 minutes
Cooking time: 15 minutes
Servings: 4

Ingredients:
- 14 oz chicken fillet
- 1 cup bread crumbs
- 2 egg yolks
- 1 teaspoon turmeric
- 1 teaspoon salt
- 1 teaspoon ginger
- 2 tablespoon cream
- 1 teaspoon olive oil

Directions:

1. Pour the olive oil in the air fryer basket.
2. Take the chicken fillet and chop it roughly.
3. Then take the mixing bowl and combine the egg yolks and salt together.
4. Whisk the mass carefully with the help of the hand whisker. Add ginger and cream and stir the mixture again gently.
5. Add turmeric and stir it again.
6. Then take the chicken pieces and dip them into the yolk mixture.
7. After this, sprinkle the chicken pieces with the bread crumbs and transfer the chicken balls in the air fryer.
8. Close the lid and cook the dish for 15 minutes.
9. Then remove the dish from the air fryer and chill it well.
10. Serve it.

Spicy potato logs

The potato logs are the best snack for your picnic outside. Make the potato logs spicy and gentle.

Prep time: 10 minutes
Cooking time: 10 minutes
Servings: 4

Ingredients:
- 3 cups mashed potato
- 1/3 cup cheddar cheese
- 1 teaspoon paprika
- 1 egg
- 1 teaspoon nutmeg
- 1 teaspoon salt
- 3 tablespoon flour
- 1 teaspoon starch

Directions:

1. Take the mixing bowl and combine the mashed potato and egg together.
2. Take the hand mixer and mix the mixture very carefully till you get smooth and homogenous mass.
3. Then sprinkle the mixture with the nutmeg, salt, paprika, and add starch. Stir it carefully again.
4. Grate the Cheddar cheese.
5. Make the small logs from the mashed potato mixture and dip the logs in the flour.
6. The sprinkle every log with the grated cheese.
7. Transfer the potato logs in the air fryer and close the lid.
8. Cook the dish for 10 minutes.
9. Then let the chill cool well and serve it immediately.

Minced meat pockets

This dish is great for your party with friends or picnic. You can change the filling of the pockets and try different variants of it.

Prep time: 15 minutes
Cooking time: 20 minutes
Servings: 6

Ingredients:
- 10 oz puff pastry
- 1 cup minced pork
- 1 white onion
- 1 teaspoon sour cream
- 1 teaspoon black pepper
- 1 teaspoon salt
- 1 teaspoon butter

Directions:

1. Take the puff pastry and roll it with the help of the rolling pin.
2. Then make the small squares from the dough.
3. Peel the onion and chop it into the tiny pieces.
4. Take the mixing bowl and combine the chopped onion and minced pork.
5. Sprinkle the mixture with the salt, black pepper, and sour cream. Stir the mass carefully.
6. Then add butter and stir it carefully again till you get smooth and homogenous mass.
7. Put the 1 teaspoon of the meat mixture in the every dough square and make the pockets from them.
8. Transfer the "pockets" in the air fryer and close the lid.
9. Cook it for 20 minutes.
10. When the dish is cooked – remove it from the air fryer and chill it well.
11. Serve the dish immediately.

Tomato circles with basil

This appetizer is a great solution for the big company of friends. It is possible to make the dish very fast.

Prep time: 10 minutes
Cooking time: 10 minutes
Servings: 4

Ingredients:
- 4 tomatoes
- 1 cup Parmesan cheese
- 4 tablespoon dry basil
- 1 teaspoon salt
- 1 teaspoon paprika
- 1 teaspoon turmeric
- 6 oz chicken fillet

Directions:

1. Wash the tomatoes very carefully and slice them into the thick circles.
2. Then chop the chicken fillet into the tiny pieces and combine it with the paprika, salt, and turmeric. Stir the mixture carefully.
3. After this, take the air fryer form and transfer the tomato circles in the basket.
4. Add the chopped chicken.
5. Grate the cheese and sprinkle the tomatoes with the grated cheese.
6. Then sprinkle the dish with the dry basil.
7. Close the lid and cook the dish for 10 minutes.
8. When the dish is cooked – chill it little and serve it immediately.

Salmon bites

The small bites are nutritious and delicious that you can serve them as for children as for adults. They are so fluffy and soft.

Prep time: 15 minutes
Cooking time: 25 minutes
Servings: 4

Ingredients:
- 1 cup butter
- 1 cup flour
- 1 teaspoon salt
- 10 oz salmon fillet
- ½ cup sour cream
- 1 tablespoon tomato sauce
- 1 teaspoon black pepper
- ¼ cup chives
- 1 cup cheddar cheese, grated

Directions:

1. Chop the butter and transfer it to the mixing bowl.
2. Sift the flour and add salt. Stir the mixture very carefully and knead the dough.
3. Then take the air fryer forms and make the small boards.
4. Chop the salmon fillet and chives.
5. Combine the chopped salmon and black pepper together. Sprinkle it with the sour cream and stir the mixture.
6. After this, chop the chives. Combine the chopped chives with the grated cheese and stir the mass.
7. Transfer the salmon fillet mixture in the boards and sprinkle them with the grated cheese mixture.
8. After this, add tomato sauce.
9. Transfer the bites in the air fryer and close the lid.
10. Cook it for 25 minutes.
11. When the dish is cooked – remove it from the air fryer and chill it well.
12. Serve it immediately.

Sausage spirals

Serve the dish only hot; otherwise, you will not get the spicy aroma and soft taste.

Prep time: 15 minutes
Cooking time: 25 minutes
Servings: 4

Ingredients:
- 10 oz yeast dough
- 8 oz sausages
- 1 teaspoon red pepper
- 1 teaspoon chili flakes
- 3 tablespoon tomato sauce
- 1 cup hard cheese
- 1 teaspoon salt
- 1 teaspoon olive oil

Directions:

1. Take the mixing bowl and combine the red pepper, chili flakes, salt, and olive oil together. Stir the mixture gently.
2. Then roll the yeast dough with the help of the rolling pin.
3. Take the sausages and chop them.
4. Grate the cheese.
5. Take the mixing bowl and combine the grated cheese and chopped sausages together. Sprinkle it with the spicy mixture and stir the mass very carefully.
6. Add tomato sauce and stir the mass again.
7. Then spread the yeast dough with the sausage mixture and roll it.
8. Cut the sausage rolls into the thick circles and transfer them in the air fryer.
9. Close the lid and cook the dish for 25 minutes.

When the dish is cooked – remove it from the air fryer and serve it hot.

Stuffed bell peppers

The bell peppers are very tender and delicious. Use the jalapeno peppers to make the dish spicy.

Prep time: 15 minutes
Cooking time: 30 minutes
Servings: 5

Ingredients:
- 5 bell peppers
- ½ cup minced chicken
- ½ cup minced beef
- 1 egg
- 1 yellow onion
- 1 teaspoon salt
- ½ cup Parmesan

Directions:

1. Wash the bell peppers carefully and cut them across into two parts. Remove the seeds from the vegetables.
2. After this, take the mixing bowl and combine the minced chicken and minced beef together. Sprinkle the mixture with the salt and add egg.
3. Stir the mass very carefully.
4. Then peel the onion and dice it.
5. Add the diced onion to the minced meat mixture and stir it very carefully.
6. Grate Parmesan cheese.
7. Transfer the minced meat mixture in the bell peppers and sprinkle them with the grated Parmesan cheese.
8. Transfer the peppers in the air fryer and close the air fryer lid.
9. Cook the dish for 30 minutes.
10. Then chill the dish briefly and serve it immediately.

Puff pastry sausages

The dish is tender and crunchy. The thick layer of the puff pastry makes you enjoy the delicious taste of the spicy sausages.

Prep time: 20 minutes
Cooking time: 30 minutes
Servings: 4

Ingredients:
- 2 garlic cloves
- 4 sausages
- 1 tablespoon sesame seeds
- 1 teaspoon ground black pepper
- 2 tablespoon olive oil
- 8 oz puff pastry
- 1 egg yolk

Directions:

1. Roll the puff pastry with the help of the rolling pin and make the squares from the dough.
2. Then peel the garlic clove and mince it.
3. Sprinkle the dough squares with the minced garlic and ground black pepper.
4. Then spray them with the olive oil.
5. Put the sausage in every square and roll them.
6. Then whisk the egg and spread the sausage rolls with the yolk mixture. Sprinkle them with the sesame seeds.
7. Transfer the dish in the air fryer and close the lid.
8. Cook the sausage rolls for 30 minutes.
9. When the dish is cooked – remove it from the air fryer and let them chill briefly,
10. Serve it immediately.

Date's rolls

The great combination of the sweet dates and bacon makes this dish incredible and delicious!

Prep time: 10 minutes
Cooking time: 15 minutes
Servings: 4

Ingredients:
- 4 bacon strips
- 4 dates
- 1/3 cup cheddar cheese
- 1 teaspoon paprika

Directions:

1. Remove the stones from the dates.
2. Then grate Cheddar cheese and combine it with the paprika. Stir the mixture.
3. Fill the dates with the cheese mixture.
4. Take the bacon strips and roll the dates in the bacon.
5. Transfer the dish in the air fryer and cook it for 15 minutes.
6. Then remove the dish from the machine and let it cool briefly.
7. Serve it immediately.

Aromatic mushroom hats

You have never tried such aromatic and delicious mushrooms hats. They are juice even after 2 days of keeping in the fridge.

Prep time: 15 minutes
Cooking time: 25 minutes
Servings: 6

Ingredients:
- 6 mushroom hats
- 1 carrot
- 1 yellow onion
- 1 tablespoon olive oil
- 1 teaspoon basil
- 1 teaspoon black pepper
- 2 tablespoon pumpkin, chopped

Directions:

1. Wash the mushroom hats very carefully.
2. Then peel the onion and carrot.
3. Dice the onion.
4. Take the carrot and grate it with the help of the grater.
5. After this combine the grated carrot and diced onion together in the mixing bowl.
6. Add olive oil, basil, and black pepper. Stir the mixture very carefully.
7. Then add pumpkin and stir it again.
8. Fill the mushroom hats with the carrot mixture.
9. Open the air fryer lid and transfer the stuffed mushroom hats in the basket.
10. Close the lid and cook the dish for 25 minutes.
11. When the dish is cooked – remove it from the air fryer and serve it immediately.

Juicy sausage buns

These juicy buns look like hot dogs but the taste it more tender and tasty. Serve the nubs only hot.

Prep time: 10 minutes
Cooking time: 7 minutes
Servings: 4

Ingredients:
- 14 oz puff pastry
- 2 eggs
- 4 sausages
- 1 teaspoon basil
- 1 teaspoon cilantro
- 1 teaspoon paprika
- 6 oz Cheddar cheese
- 1 tablespoon tomato sauce

Directions:

1. Separate the egg yolks and egg whites and put them into the separate bowls. Then whisk the egg parts gently.
2. Sprinkle the whisked egg yolk mixture with the paprika and cilantro and stir it gently.
3. After this, take the puff pastry and roll it with the help of the rolling pin.
4. Then make the medium squares from the puff pastry.
5. Spread the puff pastry squares with the egg yolk mixture carefully.
6. Put Cheddar cheese in every square and then put sausage and tomato sauce.
7. Roll the puff pastry and spread it with the whisked egg white.
8. Then sprinkle the dish with the basil.
9. Open the air fryer lid and put the sausage buns. Close the lid and cook the dish for 7 minutes. You will get the crunchy top at the end of cooking.
10. Then remove the dish from the air fryer and let it a cool little bit.
11. Serve it immediately.

Onion circles

This is the perfect snack for the big company of friends. Minimum of the oil makes this dish really healthy.

Prep time: 10 minutes
Cooking time: 8 minutes
Servings: 3

Ingredients:
- 3 big white onions
- 2 eggs
- 1 cup bread crumbs
- ½ cup wheat flour
- 1 teaspoon salt
- 1 teaspoon ground black pepper
- 1 teaspoon oregano
- ½ teaspoon hot chili pepper
- 2 tablespoon cream

Directions:

1. Peel the onions and then slice them into the thick circles. Separate every circle.
2. Take the mixing bowl and beat the eggs with it. Whisk the mixture very carefully till you get smooth and homogenous mass.
3. After this, add cream and sprinkle the liquid with the salt and black pepper. Whisk the liquid gently.
4. Then Put the flour in the separate mixing bowl and sprinkle it with the oregano and hot chili pepper. Stir it carefully.
5. Take the onion circles and dip them in the egg mixture. Then dip the circles in the flour mixture.
6. After this, dip the onions circles in the egg mixture again.
7. The last step is to dip the onion circles in the bread crumbs.
8. Open the air fryer lid and transfer the onion circles. Close the lid and cook the dish for 8 minutes.
9. When the dish is cooked – remove it from the air fryer and serve it immediately.

Air fryer lush eggs

If you do not have time for making lunch – these lush eggs will be "just right" snack or appetizer for you. The eggs are so fluffy and lush – it does not look as an omelet.

Prep time: 15 minutes
Cooking time: 10 minutes
Servings: 6

Ingredients:
- 1 teaspoon butter
- 1 cup crackers
- 1 teaspoon paprika
- ¼ cup dill
- 4 oz sausage
- ½ teaspoon baking soda
- 1 teaspoon lemon juice
- 1 teaspoon ground black pepper
- 4 eggs
- 3 tablespoon cream

Directions:

1. Take the mixing bowl and beat the eggs with it.
2. Whisk the mixture very carefully with the help of the hand whisker and add baking soda and lemon juice. Stir it gently.
3. After this, add cream and paprika. Stir the mixture carefully again.
4. Chop the sausage into the tiny pieces. Then chop the dill. Combine the chopped sausages and dill together and transfer the mixture in the egg liquid. Stir it.
5. Sprinkle the mass with the ground black pepper and stir the mixture.
6. Cover every cracker cookie with the butter.
7. Then take the air fryer muffin form and transfer the crackers in the form.
8. Pour the egg mixture in every muffin form with the cracker.
9. Transfer the muffin form in the air fryer and close the lid.
10. Cook the dish for 10 minutes.
11. When it is cooked – let it cool little and them remove the dish from the muffin forms.
12. Serve it immediately.

Parmesan chips

This delicious appetizer will stimulate your appetite before the main dish. It is also the best snack for your picnic.

Prep time: 10 minutes
Cooking time: 8 minutes
Servings: 5

Ingredients:
- 1 cup Parmesan cheese
- 1 teaspoon ground thyme
- 1 teaspoon salt
- 1 teaspoon ground black pepper
- ½ teaspoon basil

Directions:

1. Take Parmesan cheese and grate it.
2. Then sprinkle the grated Parmesan cheese with the ground thyme, salt, ground black pepper, and basil. Stir the mixture very carefully.
3. Take the air fryer form and make the circles from the Parmesan mixture.
4. Transfer the air fryer form in the air fryer and close the lid.
5. Cook the dish for 8 minutes. For this snack you do not need the oil – Parmesan is oil enough.
6. When the dish is cooked – remove it from the air fryer and chill it well till it becomes cold.
7. Serve it.

Sweet chicken bites

The Japanese style sweet chicken bites will make you cook this appetizer more and more. You can eat it before lunch or make a nutritional snack between lunch and dinner.

Prep time: 15 minutes
Cooking time: 15 minutes
Servings: 4

Ingredients:
- 15 oz chicken filler
- 1 tablespoon BBQ sauce
- 1 tablespoon sesame seeds
- 1 teaspoon salt
- 1 tablespoon lemon juice
- 1 teaspoon honey
- 1 teaspoon soy sauce
- 1 tablespoon lime zest
- 4 tablespoon chicken stock

Directions:

1. Take the chicken fillet and chop it into the medium pieces.
2. Then take the mixing bowl and combine the lemon juice, BBQ sauce, salt, honey, and soy sauce together. Stir the mixture carefully till you get smooth and homogenous mass.
3. After this, add lime zest and stir the mixture again.
4. Combine the chopped chicken and liquid mixture together in the mixing bowl and stir it carefully.
5. Leave the mass for at least 5 minutes. Then add the chicken stock and stir it again. Sprinkle the chicken with the sesame seeds and stir it gently again.
6. Open the air fryer lid and transfer the mixture in the basket. Close the lid.
7. Cook the chicken bites for 15 minutes.
8. When the dish is cooked – remove it from the air fryer and chill it till the chicken is warm.
9. Serve it immediately.

Beef puffs

It is possible to make any kind of the filling for the puffs – just find your special one!

Prep time: 20 minutes
Cooking time: 25 minutes
Servings: 5

Ingredients:
- 2 cups minced beef
- 1 white onion
- 1 cup fresh dill
- 1 egg
- 1 egg yolk
- 1 teaspoon salt
- 1 teaspoon paprika
- 1 teaspoon butter
- 1 teaspoon nutmeg
- 1 teaspoon turmeric
- 1 tablespoon lemon juice
- 15 oz puff pastry

Directions:

1. Take the mixing bowl and beat the egg. Whisk it carefully and add salt, paprika, nutmeg, turmeric, and the lemon juice. Stir the mixture.
2. After this, add the minced beef and mix up the mass carefully with the help of the hands.
3. Peel the onion and chop it. Chop the fresh dill and add the chopped ingredients in the minced meat mixture. Stir it carefully.
4. Whisk the egg yolk.
5. Take the puff pastry and roll it carefully with the help of the rolling pin. Make the medium size puff squares from the dough.
6. Then transfer the minced beef mixture in the dough squares and make the puffs.
7. Sprinkle the meat puffs with the whisked egg yolk and transfer the dish in the air fryer.
8. Cook the dish for 25 minutes.
9. When it is done – remove the puffs from the air fryer and let them cool well.
10. Serve it.

Herbed parsley balls

As usual, herbs are full of the vitamins. These delicious balls will be the best appetizer in the winter time.

Prep time: 10 minutes
Cooking time: 20 minutes
Servings: 4

Ingredients:
- 13 oz minced chicken
- 1 cup fresh parsley
- 1 tablespoon dried thyme
- 1 teaspoon salt
- 1 egg
- 1 teaspoon corn starch
- 1 teaspoon paprika
- ¼ cup fresh cilantro
- 1/3 cup flour
- ¼ cup chives

Directions:

1. Take the fresh parsley and wash it carefully. Then chop it.
2. Chop the fresh cilantro and chives.
3. After this, take the big mixing bowl and combine the chopped ingredients together.
4. Add egg and dried thyme. Stir the mixture carefully till you get homogenous mass.
5. Then sprinkle the mixture with paprika and add minced chicken. Add corn starch. Stir the mass again.
6. Add salt and stir it. Make the medium size balls from the mixture and press them little. After thus, transfer the balls in the air fryer.
7. Cook the dish for 20 minutes.
8. When it is done – serve it hot.

Potato cups

The baked potato top if the dish not only looks amazing but also very delightful. Whisk the egg white and cover the top of the dish before cooking – it will get you crunchy top.

Prep time: 20 minutes
Cooking time: 15 minutes
Servings: 6

Ingredients:
- 1 teaspoon dry yeast
- 1 cup skim milk
- 2 cups flour
- 1 cup mashed potato
- 1 onion
- 1 carrot
- ½ cup chopped chicken fillet
- 1 teaspoon sugar
- ½ teaspoon salt

Directions:

1. Take the mixing bowl and combine the dry yeast and skim milk together. Stir the mixture carefully till you get smooth mass. Then add salt and sugar and stir it again.
2. After this, sift the flour in the yeast mixture. Knead the dough and leave it.
3. Peel the onion and chop it into the tiny pieces.
4. Combine the chopped onion and mashed potato together. Stir the mixture till you get homogenous mass.
5. After this, peel the carrot and grate it with the help of the grater.
6. Take the mixing bowl and combine the grated carrot and the chopped chicken fillet together. Mix it up.
7. Then take the special air fryer forms and make the dough "cups".
8. Add the meat mixture and then add the mashed potato mass.
9. Transfer the dough cups in the air fryer and cook them for 15 minutes.
10. When the dish is cooked – remove it from the air fryer and serve it immediately.

Creamy Parmesan potatoes

This dish is appropriate to serve only in the hot way. You can sprinkle the cooked potatoes with any kinds of the chopped greens.

Prep time: 10 minutes
Cooking time: 15 minutes
Servings: 3

Ingredients:
- 3 big potatoes
- ½ cup cream
- 1 cup Parmesan
- 1/3 cup chives
- 1 teaspoon paprika
- 1 teaspoon salt
- 1 teaspoon ground black pepper
- 1 teaspoon oregano
- 1 tablespoon butter
- 1 onion

Directions:

1. Peel the onion and chop it.
2. Then wash the potatoes carefully and cut them into 2 pieces.
3. After this grate Parmesan cheese and combine it with the cream in the mixing bowl.
4. Make the boards from the potatoes by removing the meat from them.
5. Then combine the potato meat and the cheese mixture together.
6. Chop the chives and add it to the cheese mixture too.
7. After this, sprinkle the cheese mixture with the paprika, salt, ground black pepper, and oregano. Stir it carefully.
8. Then fill the potato boards with the cheese mass. Add butter on the top of every potato parts.
9. Transfer the stuffed potato parts in the air fryer and close the lid.

Cook the dish for 15 minutes. When it is cooked – serve it immediately.

Eggplant spicy toast

It is very easy and fast cook. Make this delicious for the appetizer. The eggplant spicy toasts just will emphasize your appetite.

Prep time: 15 minutes
Cooking time: 15 minutes
Servings: 4

Ingredients:
- 4 white bread slices
- 1 eggplants
- 1 teaspoon olive oil
- 2 tomatoes
- 2 garlic cloves
- 1 teaspoon basil
- 1 tablespoon grated Parmesan
- 1 teaspoon salt
- 1 teaspoon cilantro

Directions:

1. Peel the garlic cloves and mince them. After this, combine the minced garlic cloves and olive oil together.
2. Sprinkle the mixture with the basil and cilantro and stir the mixture well.
3. Then slice the eggplants into the thin pieces and rub them with salt. Leave the eggplants for at least 5 minutes.
4. Then wash the tomatoes and slice them.
5. Take the white bread slices and rub them with the garlic spicy mixture.
6. Then put the sliced tomatoes on the bread.
7. After this add sliced eggplant and sprinkle the toasts with the grated Parmesan cheese.
8. Transfer the toasts in the air fryer and close the lid.
9. Cook the toasts for 15 minutes. When the dish is cooked – let it cool briefly.
10. Serve the toast immediately.

Fish and Seafood

Fragrant mackerel

Mackerel is very soft and delicious fish. It is very nutritious and full of the vitamins. Always add the lemon sliced in the fish – it will enforce the final taste of the dish.

Prep time: 15 minutes
Cooking time: 20 minutes
Servings: 4

Ingredients:
- 4 mackerel fillets
- 3 red sweet peppers
- 1 red onion
- 1 tablespoon vinegar
- 1 zucchini
- ¼ cup parsley
- 4 garlic cloves
- 2 tablespoon olive oil
- 1 lemon
- ½ teaspoon chili flakes

Directions:

1. Peel the garlic cloves and mince them. Then peel the onion and dice it.
2. Remove the seeds from the sweet peppers and slice them.
3. Take the mixing bowl and combine all the vegetables together.
4. Sprinkle the mixture with the vinegar and olive oil. Stir the mass.
5. Take the mackerel fillet and rub it with the chili flakes. Then make the lemon zest from the lemon and squeeze the juice.
6. Combine the mixture and rub the mackerel with it. After this, chop the zucchini and parsley.
7. Combine the chopped zucchini with the chopped vegetable mixture and stir it carefully.
8. Take the air fryer form and put the vegetable mixture.
9. Then add the mackerel fillets and transfer the dish to the air fryer basket. Close the lid.
10. Cook the dish for 20 minutes.
11. When it is cooked – all the ingredients should be soft.
12. Remove the fish from the air fryer and serve it immediately.

Aromatic flounder

The main secret of the dish is the smallest amount of the oil. Always use the only orange juice for this dish; otherwise, you will not get the sour-sweet taste of the fish.

Prep time: 15 minutes
Cooking time: 15 minutes
Servings: 4

Ingredients:
- 2 teaspoon hoisin sauce
- 1 big flounder fish
- 1/3 cup chives
- 1 teaspoon ground black pepper
- 1 teaspoon white pepper
- ½ tablespoon ginger
- 1 teaspoon salt
- 1 teaspoon canola oil
- 1 small white onion
- 2 tablespoon soy sauce
- 1 teaspoon rosemary

Directions:

1. Take the mixing bowl and combine the ground black pepper, ginger, salt, and rosemary. Stir the mixture.
2. After this, take the flounder and rub it with the spicy mixture.
3. Peel the onion and chop it.
4. Combine the chopped onion and soy sauce together. Then add canola oil and hoisin sauce. Stir the mass carefully till you get homogenous mass.
5. After this, sprinkle the flounder with this mass.
6. Chop the chives.
7. Take the air fryer tray and transfer the flounder. Sprinkle it with the chopped chives from all the sides.
8. Then transfer the fish in the air fryer and cook it for 15 minutes.
9. When the dish is cooked – let it cool briefly and then transfer the fish to the serving plate.
10. Serve it.

Squid with the spicy tomato sauce

Follow the instructions of the cooking time strictly; otherwise, you will get the tough squid at the end of the cooking that is impossible to eat!

Prep time: 15 minutes
Cooking time: 10 minutes
Servings: 2

Ingredients:
- 1 cup butter beans
- 2 garlic cloves
- 1 red onion
- 1 teaspoon fresh grated ginger
- 1 teaspoon smoked paprika
- 3 tomatoes
- 1/3 cup green olives
- 1 jalapeno pepper
- 1 tablespoon tomato juice
- 1 cup fish stock
- 1 teaspoon salt
- 3 lemon wedges for serving
- 1 tablespoon orange zest
- 1 tablespoon grated parsley root
- 14 oz squid

Directions:

1. Take the mixing bowl and combine the grated parsley root, orange zest. Salt, smoked paprika and the grated ginger. Stir the mixture carefully.
2. After this, add tomato juice.
3. Dice the green olives and add the in the mixture too.
4. Then remove the seeds from the jalapeno pepper and slice it. Add the sliced jalapeno pepper in the spice mixture. Pour the fish stock.
5. After this, peel the garlic and red onion. Mince the vegetables and combine them with the butter beans.
6. Chop the tomatoes and add them to the spice mixture.
7. After this, transfer the squid to the spice mixture. Add the butter beans mixture and stir it carefully. Leave the squid for 5 minutes.
8. Then transfer it to the air fryer basket and all the liquid from the squid.
9. Close the lid and cook it for 10 minutes.
10. When the dish is cooked – stir it carefully with the help of the wooden spoon to not damaged the soft squid and serve it immediately with the lemon wedges.

Crispy trout

If you are a fan of the crispy food – this is exactly what are you looking for. Make the experiments with the spices – add the small amount of the chili pepper in the dish.

Prep time: 15 minutes
Cooking time: 15 minutes
Servings: 4

Ingredients:
- 2 eggs
- 15 oz trout
- 1/3 cup cream
- 1 cup bread crumbs
- 1 tablespoon lemon juice
- 3 tablespoon fresh ginger
- 1 teaspoon ground white pepper
- ½ teaspoon cayenne pepper
- 1 tablespoon butter
- 1 teaspoon lemon zest
- ½ teaspoon rosemary

Directions:

1. Chop the trout into the pieces.
2. Then take the big mixing bowl and beat the eggs with it. Whisk it carefully till you get smooth mass.
3. After this, add cream and bread crumbs. Stir the mixture carefully till it gets a smooth consistency.
4. After this, peel the fresh ginger and grate it. Combine the grated ginger with the lemon zest, rosemary, lemon juice and white pepper. Stir the mixture.
5. After this, melt the butter and add it to the ginger mixture. Stir it again.
6. Then pour the liquid into the bowl with chopped trout and stir it carefully. Leave it for at least 5 minutes.
7. Then dip every trout piece in the egg mixture and transfer it to the air fryer tray.
8. After this, transfer the air fryer tray in the air fryer and close it.
9. Cook the fish for 15 minutes or till it becomes crispy.
10. When the fish is cooked – remove it from the air fryer and serve it hot.

Delicious fish sticks

It is the best food for children ever. The fish sticks taste the best with the mashed potato.

Prep time: 15 minutes
Cooking time: 8 minutes
Servings: 4

Ingredients:
- 1 pound cod
- 1 teaspoon salt
- 1 teaspoon minced garlic
- 3 slices white bread
- 1 teaspoon rosemary
- 1 teaspoon oregano
- 1 teaspoon thyme
- 1 teaspoon paprika
- 1 teaspoon cilantro
- 1 egg
- 3 tablespoon four

Directions:

1. Chop the white bread slices roughly and combine them with the minced garlic. Stir it gently and transfer the mixture to the blender. Blend it carefully till you get smooth and homogenous mass.
2. Slice the cod into the sticks.
3. Take the mixing bowl and combine the cilantro, paprika, thyme, oregano, and rosemary together. Stir it gently and add flour. Stir it again.
4. After this beat the egg in the mixing bowl and whisk it.
5. Take the cod sticks and dip them in the flour mixture. After this, dip them in the egg mixture.
6. The last step is to dip the cod sticks in the bread mixture.
7. Transfer the fish sticks in the air fryer basket and close the lid.
8. Cook the dish for 8 minutes.
9. When the fish sticks are cooked – remove them from the air fryer and chill them little.
10. Serve the dish immediately.

Indian style sweet salmon

This dish is very aromatic and can amaze the most demanding gourmet. The sweet tomato sauce makes this dish incredible.

Prep time: 20 minutes
Cooking time: 15 minutes
Servings: 4

Ingredients:
- 1 tablespoon tomato sauce
- 15 oz salmon
- 1 onion
- 1 tablespoon honey
- 1 teaspoon orange juice
- 1 teaspoon lemon juice
- 1 tablespoon soy sauce
- ½ teaspoon sea salt
- 1 teaspoon olive oil
- 1 teaspoon rosemary
- 1 teaspoon fresh ginger
- ½ teaspoon coriander

Directions:

1. Slice the salmon into the portion pieces and rub them with the salt and fresh ginger.
2. Then take the mixing bowl and combine the honey, orange juice, lemon juice, soy sauce, and tomato paste. Stir the mixture very carefully till all the ingredients are dissolved and you get smooth and homogenous mass.
3. Then pour the liquid mass in the salmon and stir it gently. Leave it.
4. Meanwhile, peel the onion and chop it. Add the chopped onion in the mixing bowl with the salmon pieces. Then sprinkle the mixture with the coriander.
5. After this, transfer the salmon in the air fryer basket and sprinkle it with the olive oil. Then close the lid.
6. Cook the dish for 15 minutes.
7. When the fish is cooked – remove it from the air fryer and chill it little.
8. Serve it immediately.

Fish cutlets

What can be better than tender and juicy fish cutlets? The cutlets are very soft and can be appropriate even for toddlers.

Prep time: 15 minutes
Cooking time: 12 minutes
Servings: 5

Ingredients:
- 14 oz minced cod
- 1 teaspoon turmeric
- 1 teaspoon oregano
- 1 teaspoon basil
- 1 teaspoon salt
- 1 teaspoon sour cream
- 4 tablespoon whole grain bread
- ½ teaspoon ground white pepper
- 1 tablespoon lemon juice
- 1 teaspoon garlic powder
- 1 egg white

Directions:

1. Take the mixing bowl and combine the minced cod and egg white. Stir the mixture very carefully till you get smooth and homogenous mass.
2. After this, sprinkle the mixture with the turmeric, oregano, basil, salt, garlic powder, and ground white pepper. Stir it carefully.
3. Then add lemon juice and sour cream. Stir the mixture very carefully again and transfer it in the fridge for at least 5 minutes.
4. Meanwhile, chop the whole grain bread roughly and transfer it to the food processor. When you get smooth mass – remove it from the food processor.
5. Then remove the minced fish mixture from the fridge and make the medium cutlets from the mixture and press every cutlet little.
6. Transfer the cutlets to the air fryer basket and close the lid.
7. Cook the dish for 12 minutes. When the cutlets are cooked – remove them from the air fryer and chill them little.
8. After this, serve the cutlets immediately.

Curry sour-sweet fish

It is the traditional curry fish recipe. Follow all instructions and the final dish will exceed all your expectations

Prep time: 15 minutes
Cooking time: 15 minutes
Servings: 3

Ingredients:
- 14 oz trout
- 1 green chili
- 2 tablespoon curry paste
- 4 cups fish stock
- 1 teaspoon curry leaves
- 1 teaspoon salt
- 1 teaspoon cayenne pepper
- ½ lemon
- ½ tablespoon ginger garlic paste
- 1 teaspoon grated ginger
- 1 teaspoon turmeric
- 1 tablespoon red chili powder
- 1 teaspoon sugar

Directions:

1. Wash the trout carefully and chop the fish roughly. After this, take the mixing bowl and combine the curry paste, salt, cayenne pepper, ginger garlic paste, turmeric, and chili powder. Stir the mixture very carefully.
2. Add red chili powder and sugar and stir it again. Pour the fish stock into the mixing bowl with the curry paste mixture and stir the liquid very carefully till you get smooth and homogenous mass.
3. After this add chopped trout in the liquid and stir it. Chop the lemon. Then chop the curry leaves roughly.
4. Add the chopped ingredients in the curry paste mass and stir it gently with the help of the spoon. Then open the air fryer and transfer the fish mixture in the air fryer basket. Close the lid.
5. Cook the dish for 15 minutes. When it is ready – remove it from the air fryer and stir it gently.
6. Serve it immediately.

Snapper with shallot and tamarind sauce

The mixture of the tamarind sauce and shallot makes the fish very tender. This dish is the best choice for your family dinner.

Prep time: 15 minutes
Cooking time: 17 minutes
Servings: 4

Ingredients:
- 5-ounce snapper fillet
- 1 cup shallot
- 1 tablespoon honey
- 2 oz cilantro root
- 1 tablespoon fish sauce
- 1 red chili
- 1 tablespoon tamarind
- 1 tablespoon water
- 1 teaspoon salt
- 1 lime
- ½ cup parsley
- 1 teaspoon ground ginger
- 4 garlic cloves
- 1 green onion

Directions:

1. Rub the snapper filet with salt and leave it. After this, combine the water and tamarind together in the mixing bowl and stir it carefully till the tamarind is dissolved. Then peel the garlic cloves and onion. Mince the ingredients.
2. Grate the cilantro root. Remove the seeds from the red chili and slice it.
3. Take the big mixing bowl and combine the ingredients together.
4. Add fish sauce and ground ginger. After this, add honey. Chop the shallot and parsley. Add the chopped ingredients in the chili mixture too.
5. Transfer the snapper fillet in the air fryer basket and sprinkle it with the chili mixture. Then pour the tamarind mixture. Close the lid and cook the dish for 17 minutes.
6. Then remove the fish from the air fryer gently and chill it little. Serve it immediately with the lime wedges.

Aromatic ginger tilapia

The ginger is full of the vitamins and can enforce the delicious taste of the tilapia. You can use as fresh as dry kind of the ginger.

Prep time: 10 minutes
Cooking time: 12 minutes
Servings: 4

Ingredients:
- 1 oz fresh ginger
- 4 tilapia fillets
- 1 teaspoon thyme
- ½ teaspoon coriander
- 1 egg white
- 1 teaspoon kosher salt
- 1 tablespoon sesame oil
- 1 teaspoon minced garlic
- 2 tablespoon soy sauce

Directions:

1. Take the small mixing bowl and combine the soy sauce and the sesame oil. Stir the mixture. After this, add the minced garlic and mix up the mass.
2. Take the tilapia fillets and put them in the mixing bowl. Then pour the ginger mixture and stir it gently to not damage the fillets. Leave the fish for at least 5 minutes.
3. Meanwhile, combine the thyme, coriander, and kosher salt together in the mixing bowl.
4. Peel the ginger and grate it. Add the grated ginger in the spice mixture.
5. Whisk the egg white till you get the strong peak and add the spice mass. Stir it carefully till you get smooth and homogenous mass.
6. After this, transfer the tilapia fillet in the air fryer basket and cover it with the egg white mixture. Close the lid.
7. Cook the dish for 12 minutes.
8. When the tilapia is done – remove it from the air fryer and chill it little.
9. After this, serve the dish immediately.

Delightful scallops

The minced garlic that is included in the recipe – will make the smell and taste really delicious!

Prep time: 10 minutes
Cooking time: 7 minutes
Servings: 4

Ingredients:
- 1 pound sea scallops
- 1/3 cup garlic cloves
- 1 tablespoon lemon juice
- ½ cup butter
- 1 teaspoon paprika
- ¼ cup fresh parsley
- 1 tablespoon lemon zest
- 1 teaspoon black pepper

Directions:

1. Peel the garlic and mince it. Combine the minced garlic and lemon juice together. Stir the mixture and add lemon zest.
2. Take the big mixing bowl and combine the sea scallops and lemon mixture together. Mix it up and leave it for 5 minutes.
3. Meanwhile, chop the parsley and combine it with the paprika and black pepper. Stir the mixture.
4. After this add the chopped parsley mass in the scallops and stir it carefully again.
5. Take the butter and transfer it to the air fryer basket. Then add the scallops mixture and stir it gently.
6. Close the lid and cook the dish for 7 minutes.
7. When the scallops are cooked – remove them from the air fryer and chill them little.
8. Serve the dish!

Salmon pie

The best solution to feed the family fast is to cook this amazing creamy spinach pie. Serve the dish as hot as cold!

Prep time: 20 minutes
Cooking time: 30 minutes
Servings: 6

Ingredients:
- 10 oz salmon
- 1 cup spinach
- 14 oz puff pastry
- 1 teaspoon paprika
- 1 teaspoon salt
- 1 cup broccoli
- 1 teaspoon oregano
- 1 teaspoon basil
- 1 cup cream
- ½ teaspoon chili flakes
- 1/3 cup dill
- 1 teaspoon lemon juice
- 3 potatoes

Directions:

1. Take the salmon and mice it. Sprinkle the mixture with the salt, oregano, and basil and stir it carefully. Then chop the spinach and dill.
2. Combine the mixture together in the mixing bowl.
3. Add cream and chili flakes. Stir the mass carefully. After this, make the florets from the broccoli and chop them into the tiny pieces.
4. Peel the potatoes and grate them.
5. Sprinkle the grated potato with the lemon juice and chili flakes. Stir the mixture. Add paprika. Roll the puff pastry and transfer it in the air fryer basket.
6. Then make the filling for the pie: add the minced salmon mixture, then add the spinach mixture and broccoli.
7. After this, add grated potato mass. Cover the pie with the puff dough again and transfer the pie in the air fryer.
8. Cook the dish for 30 minutes.
9. When the pie is cooked – remove it from the air fryer and chill it till it is warm. Cut it into the pieces and serve it.

Juicy fish steak

It is very easy and tasty recipe of the fish steak. Even if you are the freshman in ccoking – you can do it!

Prep time: 20 minutes
Cooking time: 14 minutes
Servings: 2

Ingredients:
- 2 halibut fillets
- Tablespoon lime juice
- 1 handful cashew
- ½ cup green basil
- 1 teaspoon oregano
- 1 teaspoon olive oil
- 4 garlic cloves
- 1 teaspoon dry ground ginger
- 1 white onion
- 1 teaspoon sugar
- 1 teaspoon thyme
- 1 teaspoon fish sauce

Directions:

1. Take the halibut fillets and sprinkle them with the fish sauce. Then sprinkle the fish with the thyme and leave the fillet.
2. Meanwhile, take the mixing bowl and combine the cashew, oregano, and ground ginger together. Add olive oil and stir the mixture carefully. Chop the basil and add it to the mixture too.
3. After this, peel the onion and garlic cloves. Dice the vegetables and add them to the spice mixture. Mix it up.
4. Sprinkle the fish with the lemon juice and sugar.
5. Open the air fryer lid and transfer the fillets. Add the cashew mass and close the lid.
6. Cook the fish for 14 minutes.
7. When the fish is done – remove it from the air fryer carefully and chill it briefly.
8. Serve it.

Fish casserole

The dish is very light and can be appropriate for your diet plan. Use your favorite spices to enforce the final taste.

Prep time: 20 minutes
Cooking time: 18 minutes
Servings: 2

Ingredients:
- 7 ounces tilapia
- 1 egg
- ½ cup chives
- 1 white onion
- 1 cup bread crumbs
- 1 teaspoon salt
- 1 teaspoon paprika
- 1 teaspoon olive oil
- 2 potatoes
- 1/3 cup hard cheese
-

Directions:

1. Mince the tilapia and combine it with the bread crumbs in the mixing bowl.
2. Beat the egg in the mass and add olive oil. Stir it very carefully.
3. Sprinkle the fish mixture with the paprika and salt and stir it again.
4. After this, peel the onion and chop it. Add the chopped onion in the fish mixture.
5. Peel the potatoes and grate them with the help of the grater.
6. Add the grated potato in the minced fish too.
7. Grate the cheese.
8. Chop the chives and sprinkle the mixture with it.
9. Then take the air fryer tray and transfer the fish mixture into it. Sprinkle it with the grated hard cheese and transfer the tray in the air fryer. Close the lid.
10. Cook the casserole for 18 minutes. You will get the baked surface at the end of cooking.
11. Then remove the casserole from the air fryer and chill it well. Serve it.

Tilapia with tomato garlic sauce

It is a very nutritional dish that can be a great addition for your main dish. Serve the fish with the mashed potato!

Prep time: 15 minutes
Cooking time: 15 minutes
Servings: 2

Ingredients:
- 7-ounce tilapia
- 6 garlic cloves
- 4 tomatoes
- 1 cup tomato juice
- 1 tablespoon rosemary
- 1 teaspoon salt
- 1 teaspoon paprika
- 1 onion
- 1 teaspoon cayenne pepper
- 1 teaspoon ground ginger
- 1 teaspoon soy sauce

Directions:

1. Cut the tilapia into the big pieces and sprinkle the fish with the ground ginger and cayenne pepper.
2. Take the tomatoes and chop them well. Combine the chopped tomatoes and tomato juice together and transfer the mixture to the food processor.
3. Add paprika, salt, and soy sauce. Blend the mixture till you get smooth consistency or for 2 minutes.
4. Remove the liquid from the food processor.
5. Peel the onion and garlic cloves. Mince the vegetables and add them to the tomato mixture. Add rosemary and stir it carefully.
6. After this transfer the tilapia in the air fryer basket and pour the tomato garlic sauce.
7. Close the lid and cook the dish for 15 minutes.
8. When the dish is cooked – remove it from the air fryer.
9. Serve the fish with the tomato garlic sauce always!

Sriracha shrimps

The shrimps are spicy and very aromatic. It will be a great dish for your special days!

Prep time: 15 minutes
Cooking time: 9 minutes
Servings: 3

Ingredients:
- 1 pound shrimps
- 4 tablespoon sriracha
- ¼ cup fresh mint
- ¼ cup fresh rosemary
- ½ cup butter
- 1 teaspoon white pepper
- 1 teaspoon salt
- ½ teaspoon brown sugar
- 1 tablespoon soy sauce

Directions:

1. Melt the butter and combine it with the soy sauce. Stir the mixture very carefully.
2. After this, chop the rosemary and mince the fresh mint. Combine the ingredients together and add them in the butter mass.
3. Peel the shrimps and sprinkle them with the brown sugar and salt. Add white pepper and stir the mixture carefully.
4. After this add sriracha and stir it carefully again.
5. Open the air fryer lid and transfer the shrimp mixture. Add the butter sauce and stir it gently with the help of the wooden spoon.
6. Close the lid and cook the dish for 9 minutes.
7. Then remove the seafood from the air fryer and transfer it to the serving plate.
8. Ladle the fish sauce from the dish and serve it immediately.

Cod fish with the aromatic rosemary cover

It is easy, fast, and delicious recipe for the fish. Cook it and you will have the perfect dinner!

Prep time: 15 minutes
Cooking time: 15 minutes
Servings: 4

Ingredients:
- 1 pound cod
- ½ cup fresh rosemary
- 1 teaspoon white pepper
- 1 cup cream
- 1 cup fish stock
- 1 teaspoon salt
- 1 teaspoon lemon zest
- 1 teaspoon lemon juice
- 1 tablespoon fish sauce
- 1 teaspoon oregano
- 1 teaspoon basil

Directions:

1. Chop the cod into 4 fillets and sprinkle it with the lemon juice. Then rub the fish with the basil and oregano and leave it for 10 minutes.
2. Meanwhile, chop the rosemary and combine it with salt, cream, and fish stock. Stir the mixture gently.
3. Then add fish stock and lemon zest. Sprinkle the mixture with white pepper and transfer it to the blender. Blend the mass till you get smooth and homogenous mass.
4. Then transfer the cod fillets in the air fryer basket and pour the smooth cream mixture. Close the lid.
5. Cook the dish for 15 minutes.
6. Then remove the cod from the air fryer and transfer it to the serving plate. Sprinkle it with the cream mixture and serve it immediately.

Tilapia in bacon wraps with prunes

This is the fresh idea for you fish dishes. The tilapia that is cooked by this way is juicy and sweet. It is the perfect dish for your family dinner.

Prep time: 15 minutes
Cooking time: 17 minutes
Servings: 3

Ingredients:
- 3 tilapia fillets
- 3 bacon strips
- ½ cup dates pitted
- ¼ cup rosemary
- 1 teaspoon basil
- 1 teaspoon oregano
- 1 teaspoon turmeric
- ¼ cup water
- 1 teaspoon salt
- 1 teaspoon ground black pepper

Directions:

1. Take the bacon strips and sprinkle them with the ground black pepper. Stir the mixture carefully.
2. After this, rub the tilapia fillets with the basil, oregano, rosemary, and salt. Sprinkle it with the turmeric.
3. Chop the dates into the small pieces and stuff the tilapia fillets with it.
4. Then roll the tilapia fillets in the bacon strips.
5. Chop the rosemary and sprinkle the fish with it.
6. Transfer the tilapia in the air fryer and pour the water. Close the lid.
7. Cook the dish for 17 minutes.
8. Then remove it from the air fryer and serve it hot.

Crunchy mackerel with pecan and bread crumbs

This dish was invented for the special occasions. Little patient and you will get the most delicious dinner ever!

Prep time: 15 minutes
Cooking time: 15 minutes
Servings: 3

Ingredients:
- 3 mackerel fillets
- 1 handful pecan nuts
- 1 cup bread crumbs
- ¼ cup garlic
- 1 teaspoon olive oil
- 1 onion
- 6 oz hard cheese
- 1 teaspoon thyme
- 3 lemon wedges

Directions:

1. Mince the garlic and rub the mackerel fillets with the minced garlic.
2. Crush the pecan nuts and combine them with the olive oil. Then sprinkle the mixture with the bread crumbs.
3. Peel the onion and dice it.
4. Grate the hard cheese with the help of the grater and combine it with the thyme. Stir the mixture carefully.
5. After this, transfer the mackerel fillets in the air fryer basket and sprinkle them with the diced onion. Add grated cheese mixture.
6. After this, sprinkle the dish with the breadcrumbs mixture. Close the lid.
7. Cook the dish for 15 minutes.
8. Then remove the dish from the air fryer and let it cool well.
9. Serve the fish with the lemon wedges.

Stuffed trout

The dish will taste the best with the grilled vegetables garnish

Prep time: 15 minutes
Cooking time: 18 minutes
Servings: 3

Ingredients:
- 1 big trout
- 2 lime
- 1 green sweet pepper
- 1 teaspoon thyme
- 1 tablespoon lemon juice
- ½ teaspoon thyme
- 1 teaspoon sour cream
- 1 tablespoon minced garlic
- 1 teaspoon nutmeg
- 1 red onion
- 1 teaspoon sugar
- 1 teaspoon salt
- ¼ cup fish stock

Directions:

1. Rub the trout with the minced garlic, nutmeg, and thyme and leave it.
2. After this, peel the onion and chop it. Transfer the chopped onion in the mixing bowl and sprinkle it with the salt and sugar. Stir the mixture carefully.
3. After this, slice the lime into the wedges.
4. Remove the seeds from the sweet pepper and chop it. Add the chopped pepper in the onion mixture. After this, add sour cream.
5. Take the separate mixing bowl and combine the fish stock and lemon juice. Stir the mixture. Fill the trout with the onion mixture. Then add the lime wedges and transfer it in the air fryer basket.
6. Pour the fish stock mixture and close the lid.
7. Cook the fish for 18 minutes. When it is done – remove the dish from the air fryer and serve it immediately.

Tuna rice casserole

The dish is soft and tasty. This type of the casserole can substitute one of the main dishes easily!

Prep time: 15 minutes
Cooking time: 18 minutes
Servings: 3

Ingredients:
- 1-pound tuna
- 1 cup basmati rice
- 1 teaspoon fresh basil
- 1 cup cream
- 1 tablespoon starch
- 1 white onion
- 1 teaspoon dry ginger
- 2 garlic cloves
- 1 teaspoon salt
- ½ cup mushrooms
- 1 tablespoon olive oil
- 1teaspoon apple cider vinegar
- 1/3 cup hard cheese
- 2 tablespoon flour
- 1 cup fish stock

Directions:

1. Take the tuna and mince it. Transfer the minced tuna in the mixing bowl and sprinkle it with the salt and dry ginger. Stir the mixture gently.
2. After this, peel the onion and garlic clove. Dice the vegetables and add them to the tuna mixture. Sprinkle the mass with flour and starch.
3. Take the separate bowl and transfer the rice in the bowl. Pour the fish stock into the bowl and leave it.
4. Slice the mushrooms and grate the hard cheese. Sprinkle the sliced mushrooms with the apple cider vinegar and olive oil. Stir the mixture.
5. Chop the basil.
6. Then combine the tuna mixture, mushroom mixture, and rice together in the mixing bowl. Stir the mass.
7. Open the air fryer lid and transfer the mixture in the air fryer basket. Pour the cream into it and close the lid.
8. Cook the casserole for 18 minutes.
9. When the dish is done – remove it from the air fryer and chill it well. Serve it.

Salmon warm salad

This gorgeous warm fish salad will be the perfect dish for your lunch. You can add any of your favorite kind of the fish.

Prep time: 15 minutes
Cooking time: 14 minutes
Servings: 3

Ingredients:
- 1 cup green peas
- 1 pound salmon
- ½ cup fresh dill
- ¼ cup fresh celery root
- 1 tablespoon soy sauce
- 1 teaspoon lemon juice
- 1/3 cup lentils
- 2 tablespoon sour cream
- 4 tablespoon mayo, for serving
- 1 cup chicken stock

Directions:

1. Chop the salmon into the medium pieces and sprinkle the fish with the lemon juice and soy sauce. Stir the mixture well.
2. Then combine lentils and green peas together in the mixing bowl. Add sour cream and stir the mixture.
3. After this, grate the celery root and chop the fresh dill. Combine the ingredients together. Then transfer the mixture to the lentil mixture and stir it carefully.
4. Then combine the lentil mixture and salmon mixture together in the mixing bowl. Stir it very carefully.
5. Transfer the dish in the air fryer and pour the chicken stock. Stir the salad gently with the help of the spoon. Close the lid.
6. Cook the dish for 14 minutes.
7. Then remove it from the air fryer and chill it till you get a warm mixture.
8. Serve it with the mayo.

Prawn stew

If you are thinking about easy to cook and delicious dinner for your family – this stew is a great choice! It is a little bit spicy but at the same time very tender and delicious!

Prep time: 10 minutes
Cooking time: 12 minutes
Servings: 4

Ingredients:
- 5 garlic cloves
- 1 tablespoon fresh ginger
- 1 teaspoon cayenne pepper
- 9-ounce prawns
- 1 teaspoon white pepper
- ½ teaspoon chili flakes
- 1 cup basil
- 1 cup milk
- 1 tablespoon turmeric
- 1 teaspoon paprika
- 1 teaspoon salt
- 2 yellow onions

Directions:

1. Peel the onions and garlic cloves and chop the vegetables.
2. After this peel the prawns.
3. Grate the fresh ginger and combine it with the prawns. Stir the mixture.
4. Chop the basil and combine it with chili flakes, white pepper, cayenne pepper, turmeric, paprika, and salt. Stir it carefully.
5. After this, add milk in the basil mixture and stir it again.
6. Open the instant pot lid and transfer the basil mixture. Add prawns and stir it very carefully. Close the id.
7. Cook the dish for 12minutes.
8. When the stew is cooked – remove it from the air fryer and stir it very carefully again.
9. Serve it immediately.

Couscous lobster

This royal dish will amaze all your guests for sure! The millet filling makes the dish really very nutritional.

Prep time: 15 minutes
Cooking time: 18 minutes
Servings: 2

Ingredients:
- 1 lobster
- 1 cup fresh dill
- 2 garlic cloves
- 1 cup millet
- 2 tablespoon butter
- 1 teaspoon ground black pepper
- 1 teaspoon salt
- 1 teaspoon oregano
- 1 teaspoon cilantro
- 2 cups fish stock

Directions:

1. Cut the lobster across and remove the meat from the fish. Chop the meat.
2. Then take the mixing bowl and combine the chopped meat and millet. Stir it carefully and sprinkle the mixture with the salt, oregano, cilantro, and ground black pepper. Mix it very carefully.
3. Then add butter and stir it.
4. Peel the garlic cloves and chop it.
5. Fill the lobster with the millet mixture and sprinkle it with the chopped garlic.
6. Then transfer the lobster in the air fryer and pour the fish stock in the air fryer very carefully. Close the lid.
7. Cook the lobster for 18 minutes.
8. When the dish is cooked – the lobster and the filling will be soft. Remove the dish from the air fryer very carefully and transfer it to the serving plate.
9. Serve it immediately.

Crunchy Cheesy halibut

There is nothing better than crunchy fish pieces for your dinner. Serve the halibut with the fresh greens and lemon wedges.

Prep time: 15 minutes
Cooking time: 15 minutes
Servings: 4

Ingredients:
- 4 halibut fillet
- 2 tablespoon lemon juice
- 1 teaspoon olive oil
- 1 teaspoon basil
- 1 teaspoon cilantro
- 1 teaspoon ground ginger
- 1 teaspoon black pepper
- 1 tablespoon paprika
- 1 egg
- ¼ cup flour
- 1 teaspoon salt
- 1 cup bread crumbs

Directions:

1. Rub the halibut fillets with the salt, black pepper, and ground ginger. Then sprinkle the fish with the lemon juice.
2. Combine the bread crumbs, paprika, cilantro, and basil in the mixing bowl and mix the mixture up.
3. After this beat the egg in the separate bowl and whisk it. Add flour and olive oil and continue to whisk it till you get smooth and homogenous mass.
4. Then take the halibut fillets and dip them in the whisked egg mixture. Then sprinkle the fish with the breadcrumbs mixture well.
5. Transfer the fish fillets in the air fryer and close the lid.
6. Cook the dish for 15 minutes.
7. When the fish is cooked – you will get the crunchy surface of the fish – remove it from the air fryer and chill it till it is warm.
8. Serve it immediately.

Mackerel with the lentils sauce

It is the kid-friendly dish that can be great for your lunch and dinner. Use fat cream for the fish sauce.

Prep time: 20 minutes
Cooking time: 17 minutes
Servings: 3

Ingredients:
- 3 mackerel fillets
- 1 tablespoon lemon juice
- 1 tablespoon minced garlic
- 1 teaspoon thyme
- 1 teaspoon salt
- 1 cup cream
- ½ cup lentils
- 1 teaspoon dry dill
- 1 tablespoon fresh parsley
- 1egg

Directions:

1. Chop the mackerel roughly and transfer it to the mixing bowl. Sprinkle the fish with the lemon juice and minced garlic. Stir it carefully and leave the mixture.
2. Then combine the cream with the thyme, lentils, and dry dill. Stir the mixture.
3. Take the separate bowl and beat the egg. Add salt and whisk it carefully.
4. Chop the parsley and add it in the whisked egg. Pour the egg mixture over the fish and stir it carefully till you get homogenous mass.
5. Then transfer the fish in the air fryer and pour the cream mixture. Close the air fryer lid and cook the dish for 17 minutes.
6. When the fish is cooked – do not stir it anymore. Remove it from the air fryer and serve it immediately.

Salmon fritters

These fritters do not consist vegetable oil. The big amount of the fresh spinach makes the dish really useful.

Prep time: 15 minutes
Cooking time: 13 minutes
Servings: 4

Ingredients:
- 3 cups minced salmon
- 1 ½ cup spinach
- 1 egg
- 1 teaspoon salt
- 1 teaspoon oregano
- 1 tablespoon basil
- ½ tablespoon cornstarch
- 1 tablespoon cream
- 1 tablespoon minced garlic
- 1 teaspoon paprika

Directions:

1. Take the mixing bowl and beat the egg in the bowl. Whisk the mixture very carefully till you get homogenous mass. Then sprinkle the whisked egg with the salt, oregano, cornstarch, and minced garlic. Stir it gently again.
2. After this, add paprika and cream. Stir it carefully.
3. Chop the spinach into the tiny pieces. You can use the hand blender for this step.
4. Add the chopped spinach in the egg mixture and stir it carefully again.
5. After this, add minced salmon and knead the dough for the fritters.
6. Make the round fritters and press them little.
7. Transfer the fritters in the air fryer and close the lid.
8. Cook them for 13 minutes.
9. Then remove the cooked fritters from the air fryer and chill them well.
10. Serve the dish immediately.

Seafood pizza

This pizza can contain any of your favorite seafood. Sprinkle the dish with the lemon juice before serving – it will give the perfect taste.

Prep time: 15 minutes
Cooking time: 20 minutes
Servings: 3

Ingredients:
- 7 oz pizza dough
- 1 cup prawns
- ½ cup clams
- ½ cup fresh dill
- 1 tablespoon sour cream
- 1 tablespoon tomato sauce
- 1 teaspoon minced garlic
- 1 teaspoon salt
- 1 teaspoon soy sauce
- 2-ounce salmon
- 1 tablespoon lemon juice

Directions:

1. Peel the prawns. Take the mixing bowl and combine the peeled prawns and claims together with it. Sprinkle it with the soy sauce and stir the mixture gently.
2. After this, chop the salmon roughly and add the chopped fish in the mixture too.
3. Sprinkle the mass with the minced garlic, salt, and lemon juice. Stir it carefully.
4. After this, chop the dill.
5. Roll the pizza dough with the help of the rolling pin.
6. Combine the tomato sauce and sour cream together in the mixing bowl and stir it carefully till you get homogenous mass.
7. Spread the pizza dough with the mass and the sprinkle it with the S of the chopped dill.
8. Transfer the seafood mixture in the pizza dough and sprinkle it with the chopped dill again.
9. Transfer the pizza to the air fryer basket and close the lid.
10. Cook the dish for 20 minutes or till it is done.
11. Serve it hot.

Seafood salad with noodles

This salad is appropriate to eat as cold as warm. It is better to connect 2 types of the seafood for the salad.

Prep time: 15 minutes
Cooking time: 14 minutes
Servings: 4

Ingredients:
- 8 oz rice noodles
- 3 cup chicken stock
- 1 cup scallops
- 1 cup shrimps
- 1 tablespoon lemon juice
- 1teaspoon soy sauce
- 1teapsoon salt
- 1 teaspoon oregano
- 1 teaspoon basil
- 1 teaspoon paprika
- ½ teaspoon cayenne pepper
- 1 tablespoon apple cider vinegar
- 1 carrot
- 1 cucumber, for serving

Directions:

1. Transfer the rice noodles in the air fryer basket. Peel the carrot and make the spirals with the help of the spiralizer. Then peel the shrimps and chop them roughly. Add the spiraled carrot and seafood in the air fryer too.
2. Combine the apple cider vinegar, cayenne pepper, paprika, basil, salt, soy sauce, and lemon juice together. Stir the mixture and add the chicken stock. Stir it carefully again.
3. Then pour the liquid into the air fryer and close the lid. Cook the dish for 14 minutes. Meanwhile, slice the cucumber.

When the dish is cooked – remove it from the air fryer and sprinkle it with the sliced cucumber. Serve it immediately.

Seafood pie

There is no need to buy expensive and rare seafood for this dish – just combine two types of the fish – and you will get the delicious flavor!

Prep time: 10 minutes
Cooking time: 30 minutes
Servings: 3

Ingredients:
- ½ cup salmon
- 1/3 cup halibut
- 1 egg
- 1 cup cream
- 1 cup flour
- 1 teaspoon salt
- 1 teaspoon paprika
- 1 teaspoon baking soda
- ½ teaspoon basil
- ½ teaspoon oregano
- 1 teaspoon cilantro
- 1 onion
- ½ teaspoon turmeric

Directions:

1. Peel the onion and chop it into the tiny pieces. Chop the halibut and the salmon into the same pieces as the onion. Take the mixing bowl and combine all the ingredients together. Sprinkle the mixture with the salt, paprika, basil, oregano, cilantro, and turmeric. Stir it carefully again.
2. After this, take the separate bowl and beat the egg. Whisk it carefully.
3. Add the cup of cream, flour, and baking soda. Mix up the mass with the help of the hand mixer. After this, take the air fryer form and pour the S of the dough. Add all fish mixture. Then pour the second part of the dough.
4. Transfer the pie in the air fryer and close the lid. Cook it for 30 minutes. When the pie is cooked – remove it from the air fryer, chill it little and serve it immediately.

Poultry

Chicken casserole

This delicious chicken casserole will be a great decision for your dinner. The final dish is very soft and aromatic.

Prep time: 20 minutes
Cooking time: 20 minutes
Servings: 6

Ingredients:
- 9-ounce chicken fillet
- 2 white onions
- 1 teaspoon thyme
- 1 teaspoon coriander
- 1teaspoon basil
- 2 carrots
- ½ cup celery
- 1/3 cup bread crumbs
- 1 teaspoon salt
- 2 sweet potatoes
- ½ cup broccoli
- 1 cup cream
- 1 cup chicken stock

Directions:
1. Take the chicken fillet and cut it into the strips. Sprinkle the chicken strips with the salt and basil stir the mixture. Wash the carrot carefully and peel it. Slice the carrot. Peel the onions and dice them. Then peel the sweet potato and chop it. Chop the celery. Wash the broccoli carefully.
2. Take the mixing bowl and combine all the vegetables together. Stir the mixture and add coriander and thyme. Stir it.
3. Transfer the chicken strips into the air fryer basket and add vegetables. Pour the mixture with cream and stir it gently. Sprinkle the casserole with the bread crumbs. After this, add chicken stock and close the lid.
4. Cook the dish for 20 minutes. When the dish is cooked – serve it immediately.

Chicken neck soup with dumplings

You have never tried such type of soup. The potato was substitute with the dumplings that make the soup really nutritious and delightful.

Prep time: 20 minutes
Cooking time: 18 minutes
Servings: 6

Ingredients:
- 5 cups chicken stock
- 1 cup flour
- 14 oz chicken necks
- 1 onion
- 1 egg
- 1 teaspoon salt
- ½ teaspoon baking soda
- ½ cup water
- 1 carrot
- 1 cup fresh dill
- 1 bay leaf
- ½ teaspoon rosemary
- 1 tablespoon sour cream
- 1 teaspoon paprika

Directions:
1. Take the mixing bowl and beat the egg. Whisk it carefully and add water. Stir it gently.
2. After this, combine the flour and baking soda together and transfer the mixture in the whisked egg. Sprinkle it with salt and knead the dough. Leave it.
3. Peel the onion and carrot and chop the vegetables.
4. Chop the dill and combine it with the chopped vegetables in the mixing bowl. Stir it carefully.
5. After this. Transfer the chicken necks in the air fryer and add vegetable mixture. Pour the mass with the chicken stock. Add dill mixture, bay leaf, rosemary, paprika, and sour cream.
6. Make the small balls (dumplings) from the dough and add them to the air fryer basket too.
7. Close the lid and cook the dish for 18 minutes. When the soup is done transfer it to the serving bowls carefully and serve it immediately.

Chicken Marsala

If you try this dish once – you will want to cook it again and again. The taste of the chicken is delicious and the smell is aromatic.

Prep time: 10 minutes
Cooking time: 20 minutes
Servings: 4

Ingredients:
- ¾ cup marsala
- 1 cup mushrooms
- 2 chicken breast, skinless
- 2 cup chicken stock
- ½ cup flour
- 2 tablespoon butter
- 1 teaspoon salt
- 1 teaspoon ground black pepper
- 1 teaspoon garlic powder
- ½ teaspoon onion powder
- 1 teaspoon thyme
- 1 bay leaf
- ½ teaspoon cayenne pepper

Directions:

1. Chop the chicken breasts roughly.
2. Take the mixing bowl and combine flour, garlic powder, onion powder, thyme, and cayenne pepper together in the mixing bowl. Toss the chopped chicken breasts and stir it carefully. Then remove the breasts from the flour mixture and transfer them in the air fryer basket.
3. Slice the mushrooms and sprinkle them with the salt, ground black pepper, and butter. Stir it carefully. Add the sliced mushrooms in the air fryer basket too,
4. Then add bay leaf, Marsala, and chicken stock. Stir it carefully.
5. Close the lid and cook the dish for 20 minutes.
6. When it is done – remove it from the air fryer and serve it immediately.

Nutritional chicken stew with gnocchi

This dish is kid-friendly. It is very soft and can be appropriate even for toddlers.

Prep time: 15 minutes
Cooking time: 20 minutes
Servings: 4

Ingredients:
- 2 carrots
- 1 cup mashed potato
- 3 tablespoon flour
- 1 egg
- 1 teaspoon salt
- 4 chicken fillets
- 1 onion
- ½ cup fresh dill
- 1 teaspoon oregano
- 1 teaspoon cilantro
- 1 teaspoon minced garlic
- 1 teaspoon ginger
- 2 cup chicken stock

Directions:

1. Make the gnocchi: combine the flour and mashed potato together and stir it carefully. Then beat the egg in the mixture and add salt. Stir it carefully till you get homogenous mass. Knead the dough.
2. Chop the fillet into the medium pieces. Sprinkle the meat with the cilantro, oregano, minced garlic, and ginger. Stir it carefully.
3. Peel the onion and carrot and dice the vegetables.
4. Transfer the chopped meat. Dice onion and carrot in the air fryer and pour chicken stock.
5. Make the gnocchi from the mashed potato mass and transfer them in the air fryer basket too.
6. Close the lid and cook the dish for 20 minutes.
7. Then remove it from the air fryer, chill it little, stir it, and serve immediately.

Hot and spicy chicken with the BBQ sauce

This chicken will be a great choice for your picnic at home. No need to go outside – just follow all the directions and you will get perfect picnic dish.

Prep time: 10 minutes
Cooking time: 14 minutes
Servings: 3

Ingredients:
- 3 tablespoon BBQ sauce
- 3 chicken fillets
- ½ cup black olives
- 1 onion
- 1 tablespoon tomato sauce
- 1 teaspoon cayenne pepper
- ½ teaspoon hot chili pepper
- 1 teaspoon olive oil
- 1 teaspoon salt
- 2 tablespoon minced garlic
- ¾ cup soy sauce
- ¾ cup chicken stock

Directions:

1. Take the mixing bowl and combine the soy sauce and chicken stock. Stir the mixture.
2. Take the chicken fillets and rub them with the cayenne pepper, hot chili pepper, and salt. Then sprinkle the meat with the olive oil.
3. Slice the black olives.
4. Take the small mixing bow and combine the BBQ sauce and tomato sauce. Stir it carefully.
5. Peel the onion and dice it. Combine the diced onion and minced garlic together. Then combine the mixture with the chicken fillets.
6. Transfer the chicken to the air fryer basket and pour the soy sauce mixture. Add the BBQ sauce mass and sprinkle the meat with the sliced black olives.
7. Close the lid and cook the dish for 14 minutes.
8. When the meat is cooked – do not stir it and remove it from the air fryer.
9. Serve it immediately with the juice from the chicken.

Thai style chicken with teriyaki sauce

It is the most popular Japanese dish that can be cooked very easy. You will be amazed by the thin taste of the cooked chicken.

Prep time: 15 minutes
Cooking time: 20 minutes
Servings: 4

Ingredients:
- 4 chicken tights
- 1 cup soy sauce
- 1 tablespoon sugar
- 1 tablespoon cooking sake
- 1 teaspoon sesame seeds
- 1 tablespoon tomato sauce
- 1 teaspoon honey
- 4 tablespoon chicken stock

Directions:

1. Pour the chicken stock in the air fryer basket.
2. Take the mixing bowl and combine the soy sauce, sugar, honey, cooking sake, and tomato sauce. Stir the mixture carefully till you get smooth and homogenous mass.
3. After this, transfer the chicken tights in the sauce and stir the mass carefully.
4. Sprinkle the chicken with the sesame seeds and stir it again. Leave the chicken for at least 5 minutes.
5. Then transfer the meat in the air fryer basket and pour the sauce in the air fryer basket too. Close the lid.
6. Cook the dish for 20 minutes.
7. Then remove the dish from the air fryer and serve it immediately.

Butter chicken

This delightful Indian dish is not difficult to cook! You can try it for your lunch or family dinner – be sure you will be satisfied with the result! This is the fast recipe of cooking this dish.

Prep time: 15 minutes
Cooking time: 18 minutes
Servings: 4

Ingredients:
- 14 oz chicken
- 1 teaspoon salt
- 1 teaspoon red chili pepper
- 1 tablespoon lemon juice
- ½ teaspoon turmeric
- 1 teaspoon garam masala powder
- 1 teaspoon olive oil
- 1 teaspoon ginger-garlic paste
- 1/3 cup Greek yogurt
- 3 tablespoon butter
- 1 teaspoon cardamom
- 1 clove
- 1 coriander leaf
- 1 teaspoon sugar
- ½ cup cream

Directions:

1. Chop the chicken roughly and transfer it to the mixing bowl. Sprinkle the meat with the salt, red chili pepper, and lemon juice. Stir it carefully.
2. Then add turmeric, garam masala powder. And olive oil. Stir the mixture carefully again.
3. After this, add ginger-garlic paste and cardamom.
4. Take the separate bowl and combine Greek yogurt and butter. Stir the mixture carefully till you get smooth and homogenous mass. Add the coriander leaf and sugar. Then add clove and stir the mixture carefully. Add cream.
5. Transfer the chicken mixture in the air fryer basket and pour it with the Greek yogurt mass. Close the lid.
6. Cook the dish for 18 minutes.
7. When the dish is done – stir it carefully and transfer it to the serving plates.
8. Serve it immediately.

Chicken enchiladas

It is very fast to cook the chicken dish. It is the best choice for your late dinner.

Prep time: 20 minutes
Cooking time: 16 minutes
Servings: 4

Ingredients:
- 4 chicken fillets
- 4 tortillas
- 2 white onions
- 1 cup cream
- 1 tablespoon Greek yogurt
- 2 cups Cheddar cheese
- 1 cup pickle cucumbers
- 1 teaspoon black pepper
- 1 teaspoon minced garlic
- 2 tablespoon tomato sauce
- 1 tablespoon sour cream
- 1 teaspoon salt
- 1 teaspoon chili flakes
- 1 cup lettuce
- 1 teaspoon parsley

Directions:

1. Take the chicken fillets and cut it into the strips. Then cut every strip into 2 parts more.
2. Transfer the meat to the mixing bowl and sprinkle it with the parsley, salt, black pepper, and the minced garlic. Stir the mixture carefully.
3. Take the separate bowl and combine Greek yogurt, sour cream, tomato sauce, and chili flakes.
4. Stir the mixture very carefully till you get homogenous mass.
5. Then grate Cheddar cheese and dice the pickled cucumber.
6. Peel the onion and chop it.
7. Take the tortillas and spread it with the Greek yogurt mixture carefully.
8. Then transfer the chicken strips in the tortillas, add diced pickled cucumber. Add chopped onion. Then sprinkle the dish with the Cheddar cheese and roll it.
9. Transfer the tortillas to the air fryer basket and pour the cream. Close the lid and cook the dish for 16 minutes.
10. When the dish is cooked – remove it from the air fryer basket carefully and serve it immediately.

Chicken with artichokes

This is the most delicious recipe for the chicken you ever tried. The main secret of the dish is in well-spiced artichokes.

Prep time: 15 minutes
Cooking time: 17 minutes
Servings: 4

Ingredients:
- 8 chicken tights
- 2 white onions
- 10-ounce artichoke hearts
- 1/3 cup parsley
- 1 teaspoon ground black pepper
- 1 teaspoon white pepper
- 1/3 cup sour cream
- ¾ cup mayonnaise
- 1 cup chicken stock
- 1 teaspoon turmeric
- 1 tablespoon grated fresh ginger
- 1 teaspoon paprika
- 1 teaspoon butter

Directions:

1. Chop the chicken tight roughly and transfer them to the mixing bowl. Sprinkle it with the ground black pepper, white pepper, turmeric, and grated fresh ginger. Stir the mixture every carefully.
2. Take the separate bowl and combine the chicken stock, butter, mayonnaise, and the sour cream. Stir the mixture very carefully till you get smooth mass.
3. After this, pour the mixture in the chicken mass and leave it.
4. Finally, chop the artichokes hearts. Peel the onion and chop it too.
5. Chop the parsley and combine it with the paprika and chopped onion.
6. Combine the meat, chopped artichokes, and the onion mixture together and transfer it to the air fryer basket. Close the lid. Cook it for 17 minutes.
7. When the dish is cooked –remove it from the air fryer and serve it immediately.

Chicken cordon bleu

The chicken is very soft and will melt in your mouth! Serve the dish only hot.

Prep time: 15 minutes
Cooking time: 18 minutes
Servings: 4

Ingredients:
- 4 chicken fillets
- 5-ounce hard cheese
- 4 eggs
- ½ cup flour
- 1 cup bread crumbs
- 4 slices of ham
- 4 teaspoon butter
- 1 teaspoon salt
- 1 teaspoon paprika

Directions:

1. Take the mixing bowl and sift the flour. Add eggs and mix the mixture up very carefully till you get smooth and homogenous mass.
2. Then take the chicken fillets and beat them well.
3. Rub the chicken fillets with the salt and paprika. Then add the ham and hard cheese in every fillet. Add butter.
4. Seal close the chicken fillets with the toothpick and dip them in the flour-egg mixture.
5. Then dip the chicken in the breadcrumbs.
6. Transfer the chicken in the air fryer and close the lid.
7. Cook the dish for 18 minutes.
8. When it is cooked – remove it from the air fryer and discard the toothpick from the dish.
9. Serve it hot!

Honey chicken wings

You can cook this dish for your outside lunch on the weekend or take it for the family Picnic. The meat is very tender and not spicy at all.

Prep time: 15 minutes
Cooking time: 15 minutes
Servings: 4

Ingredients:
- 16 chicken wings
- 1 tablespoon honey
- 2 teaspoon soy sauce
- 1 tablespoon tomato sauce
- 1 teaspoon minced garlic
- 1 tablespoon brown sugar
- 3 tablespoon butter
- 1 teaspoon salt
- ½ cup cilantro
- 1 tablespoon lemon juice
- 1 teaspoon apple cider vinegar

Directions:

1. Take the mixing bowl and combine honey, soy sauce, tomato sauce, and minced garlic. Stir the mixture carefully till you get homogenous mass.
2. Then add the chicken wings in the mixing bowl and mix the mass up. Leave it.
3. Wash the cilantro and chop it roughly. Transfer the chopped cilantro in the food processor and start to blend it till you get smooth mass.
4. Then add lemon juice and salt. Sprinkle the mixture with the apple cider vinegar. Add butter and brown sugar. Blend it for 30 seconds more.
5. Then ladle the mixture in the wings mixture and stir it carefully again.
6. After this, transfer the chicken wing's mixture in the air fryer basket and close the lid.
7. Cook the dish for 15 minutes.
8. When the chicken is cooked – remove it from the air fryer basket and chill it little.
9. Serve it.

Chicken breast with prunes and cilantro

The chicken has the sweet and sour taste. Serve the dish with the curry rice.

Prep time: 15 minutes
Cooking time: 15 minutes
Servings: 2

Ingredients:
- 2 chicken breasts
- ½ cup prunes
- 1 cup cilantro
- ½ cup dried tomatoes
- 1 tablespoon butter
- 1 teaspoon salt
- 1 teaspoon paprika
- 1 teaspoon basil
- 1 tablespoon olive oil
- 1 cup cream

Directions:

1. Take the chicken breasts and cut them across.
2. Rub the meat with the basil, paprika, and salt.
3. Then chop the prunes and dried tomatoes.
4. Chop the cilantro and combine all the chopped ingredients together.
5. Transfer the mixture in the chicken breasts. Add butter and seal the chicken close with the toothpicks. Then rub the chicken with the olive oil.
6. Transfer the chicken breasts in the air fryer basket and pour the cream.
7. Cook the dish for 15 minutes.
8. When it is done – remove it from the air fryer – chill it till it is warm and serve it immediately.

Stuffed chicken breast with herbs and mushrooms

This is real autumn dish! The gentle taste of the mushrooms makes this dish unforgettable.

Prep time: 15 minutes
Cooking time: 17 minutes
Servings: 2

Ingredients:
- 1 cup chestnut mushrooms
- 1 yellow onion
- ½ cup butter
- 1 teaspoon thyme
- 1 teaspoon coriander
- 1 teaspoon oregano
- 2 tablespoon cream
- 1 teaspoon garlic
- 1 tablespoon minced ginger
- 1 teaspoon dry dill
- 1 cup chicken stock
- 1 big chicken breast

Directions:

1. Take the mixing bowl and transfer the butter. Add thyme, oregano, coriander, and garlic. Stir the mixture very carefully till you get smooth and homogenous mass.
2. After this, combine cream with the dry dill and minced ginger. Stir the mass.
3. Peel the onion and chop it.
4. Wash the chestnut mushrooms very carefully and slice them.
5. Cut the chicken breast across and transfer the mushrooms and butter mixture. Seal the breast close with the toothpicks.
6. Transfer the chicken breast in the air fryer basket and pour the cream mixture. Close the lid.
7. Cook the dish for 17 minutes.
8. When the chicken is cooked – remove it from the air fryer and chill it well. Cut it into the pieces.
9. Serve it immediately.

Chicken divan

You can substitute the chicken tights with the fillets and breasts.

Prep time: 15 minutes
Cooking time: 16 minutes
Servings: 2

Ingredients:
- 1 cup quinoa
- 1 carrot
- 1 cup broccoli
- 10-ounce chicken
- 1 cup shallot
- 2 cups chicken stock
- 1 cup water
- ½ cup hard cheese
- 1 tablespoon white wine
- 1 teaspoon nutmeg
- 1 teaspoon salt
- ½ teaspoon sugar
- 1 onion

Directions:

1. Chop the chicken into the medium pieces and sprinkle it with the salt and nutmeg. Stir the mixture.
2. Peel the onion and chop it. Slice the shallot.
3. Wash the broccoli carefully and separate it into the florets. Then chop it into the tiny pieces.
4. Take the mixing bowl and transfer the chopped broccoli in the bowl.
5. Add the sliced shallot and chopped onion. Then add quinoa.
6. Grate the cheese.
7. After this, transfer the quinoa mass in the chicken mixture and add grated cheese. Stir it very carefully and transfer the mixture in the air fryer basket.
8. Pour the chicken stock and water in the air fryer basket and close the lid. Add wine. Cook the dish for 16 minutes.
9. When it is done – remove it from the air fryer and stir it very carefully. Serve it.

Curry chicken

It is a very simple rustic recipe of the chicken. You can serve it with rice for the dinner.

Prep time: 15 minutes
Cooking time: 15 minutes
Servings: 4

Ingredients:
- 1 cup chives
- 12-ounce chicken fillet
- 1 cup chicken stock
- 1 tablespoon curry paste
- ½ tablespoon garam masala
- 1 onion
- 1 tablespoon cream
- 1 tablespoon flour
- 1 teaspoon minced garlic
- 1 tablespoon minced fresh ginger
- 1 teaspoon dry celery root

Directions:

1. Cut the chicken fillet into the strips and sprinkle it with the garam masala. Stir the mixture very carefully and add curry paste. Stir it again.
2. Take the separate bowl and combine the dry celery root, minced fresh ginger, and minced garlic together. Stir it carefully and add flour and cream. Then add chicken stock and mix up the mass carefully till you get smooth and homogenous mass.
3. After this, chop the chives.
4. Transfer the chicken strips in the air fryer, sprinkle the mixture with the chopped chives and pour the chicken stock liquid. Close the lid.
5. Cook the dish for 15 minutes.
6. When the chicken is cooked – remove it from the air fryer and transfer it to the serving bowls, ladle the juice from the chicken and serve it immediately.

Buffalo chicken

The taste of the dish is the same as you tried in your favorite restaurant! You can use any kind of the chicken for this recipe.

Prep time: 15 minutes
Cooking time: 15 minutes
Servings: 5

Ingredients:
- 12-ounce chicken
- 2 tablespoon hot sauce
- 1 teaspoon olive oil
- 1 tablespoon onion powder
- 1 teaspoon garlic powder
- 1 teaspoon salt
- ½ teaspoon cayenne pepper
- 1 teaspoon turmeric
- 1 teaspoon paprika
- 4 tablespoon chicken stock

Directions:

1. Wash the chicken carefully and chop it coarsely. Sprinkle the chopped chicken with the salt, cayenne pepper, onion powder, garlic powder, paprika, and turmeric. Stir the mixture very carefully.
2. After this, take the shallow bowl and combine the olive oil, hot sauce, and chicken stock. Stir the liquid carefully till you get homogenous mass.
3. After this, pour the hot sauce liquid in the chicken mixture and stir it again.
4. Then transfer the chicken in the air fryer and close the lid.
5. Cook the dish for 15 minutes.
6. When the chicken is cooked – chill it well till the dish is warm and serve it immediately.

Chicken nuggets

The nuggets can be healthy food too! Make this delicious dish and your children will fall in love with it for sure!

Prep time: 10 minutes
Cooking time: 8 minutes
Servings: 2

Ingredients:
- 10 oz chicken fillet
- 1 cup bread crumbs
- 1 egg
- 1 teaspoon salt
- 1 teaspoon basil
- 1 teaspoon turmeric
- 1 tablespoon cream
- 1 tablespoon flour

Directions:

1. Wash the chicken fillet carefully and chop it coarsely.
2. Sprinkle the fillet with the salt and stir it.
3. Take the shallow bowl and combine the turmeric and basil. Stir the mixture.
4. After this, take the separate bowl and beat the egg in the bowl. Whisk it carefully and add cream and flour. Stir it carefully till you get smooth mass.
5. Then dip the chicken in the egg mixture carefully.
6. Combine the bread crumbs and the turmeric mixture together. Dip the chicken nuggets in the bread crumbs carefully.
7. After this, transfer the dish in the air fryer and close the lid.
8. Cook it for 8 minutes.
9. Then remove the chicken nuggets from the air fryer and serve them hot!

Chicken legs with lemon spicy sauce

Firstly, you will be amazed by the delicious aroma of the dish and then fall in love with its taste!

Prep time: 15 minutes
Cooking time: 15 minutes
Servings: 2

- 4 chicken legs
- 1 lemon
- 1 tablespoon lemon zest
- 1 teaspoon cayenne pepper
- S teaspoon red chili pepper
- 1 teaspoon hot sauce
- 1 teaspoon chopped parsley
- 1 teaspoon oregano
- 1 teaspoon honey

Directions:

1. Cut the lemon into two parts and squeeze the juice.
2. Combine the lemon juice and lemon zest together. Add red chili pepper, hot sauce, oregano, and honey. Stir the mixture carefully till you get homogenous mass.
3. Slice the lemon into the wedges and transfer the wedges to the lemon mixture. Stir it again.
4. Then add the chicken legs and mix the mixture up very carefully.
5. After this, transfer the chicken legs with all liquid in the air fryer and close the lid.
6. Cook the dish for 15 minutes.
7. When the chicken legs are cooked – remove them from the air fryer and serve the dish immediately.

Crunchy chicken fillet

The crunchy chicken can be tasty and healthy. These chicken fillets have the most delicious smell ever.

Prep time: 15 minutes
Cooking time: 9 minutes
Servings: 4

Ingredients:
- 2 chicken fillets
- 10 oz Parmesan cheese
- 1 tablespoon soy sauce
- 1 teaspoon honey
- 1 teaspoon dry ginger
- 1 teaspoon paprika
- 1 tablespoon dry French parsley

Directions:

1. Take the chicken fillets and slice them into 4 parts. Rub the fillets with the dry ginger and paprika.
2. Then add soy sauce and honey. Mix up the mass carefully and leave it for 10 minutes.
3. Grate the parmesan cheese.
4. Then sprinkle the meat with the dry French parsley and transfer it in the air fryer basket. Sprinkle the meat with the grated cheese gently.
5. Cook it for 9 minutes.
6. When the dish is cooked – remove it from the air fryer and chill it till the chicken is warm.
7. Serve it.

Garlic chicken wings

The dish tastes the best with the sour-sweet sauce. Serve the wings with the mashed potato.

Prep time: 15 minutes
Cooking time: 14 minutes
Servings: 4

Ingredients:
- 8 chicken wings
- ½ cup garlic cloves
- 1 tablespoon sour cream
- 1 tablespoon lime zest
- 1 teaspoon curry
- 1 tablespoon fish sauce
- 1 teaspoon butter

Directions:

1. Combine the fish sauce and butter together and whisk the mixture. Add curry and sour cream and stir the mixture carefully till you get homogenous mass.
2. After this transfer, the chicken wings in the mixture and sprinkle it with the lemon zest.
3. Then peel the garlic cloves and slice them. Transfer the sliced garlic in the chicken wings mixture and stir it gently. Leave the mass for at least 5 minutes.
4. Then transfer the chicken mixture in the air fryer and close the lid.
5. Cook the dish for 14 minutes.
6. When the dish is cooked – remove it from the air fryer and discard the liquid from the chicken wings.
7. Serve the wings immediately.

Chicken piccata

This dish will be good only for adults. It consists of wine!

Prep time: 15 minutes
Cooking time: 15 minutes
Servings: 4

Ingredients:
- 4 chicken fillet
- 1 lemon
- ½ cup parsley
- ½ cup cream
- ¾ cup white wine
- 1 teaspoon nutmeg
- 1 teaspoon ground black pepper
- 1/3 cup capers
- 1/3 cup flour
- 2 eggs
- ¾ cup chicken stock
- 2 teaspoon paprika

Directions:

1. Take the big mixing bowl and beat the eggs with it. Whisk the mixture carefully.
2. After this, add cream and stir it gently.
3. Then sprinkle the mixture with the paprika and stir it.
4. Beat the chicken fillets gently and transfer them to the egg mixture.
5. Then dip the fillets in the flour.
6. Take the separate bowl and combine capers, ground black pepper, white wine, and chicken stock. Stir it.
7. Pour this mixture into the air fryer and then transfer the chicken fillets.
8. Close the lid and cook the dish for 15 minutes.
9. Chop the parsley.
10. Then remove it from the air fryer. Transfer the fillets in the serving plates and sprinkle them with capers. Sprinkle the dish with the chopped parsley.
11. Serve it immediately.

Sweet duck fillet

The duck meat will be gentle if you add the apple cider vinegar in the marinade.

Prep time: 20 minutes
Cooking time: 17 minutes
Servings: 6

Ingredients:
- 2 duck breasts
- 1 cup tomato juice
- 1 tablespoon apple cider vinegar
- 1 teaspoon brown sugar
- 2 tablespoon honey
- 1 teaspoon soy sauce
- 2 teaspoon minced garlic
- 1 carrot
- ½ cup green olives

Directions:

1. Cut the duck breasts into 2 parts.
2. Take the big mixing bowl and combine the tomato juice, apple cider vinegar, brown sugar, honey, and soy sauce together. Stir the mixture carefully till all the ingredients are dissolved.
3. After this, add minced garlic.
4. Peel the carrot and make the spirals with the help of the spiralizer.
5. Add the spiralized carrot in the tomato mixture. Stir it gently.
6. Transfer the chicken breasts to the tomato mixture and mix it up.
7. Leave the mass for at least 5 minutes.
8. Meanwhile, slice the green olives.
9. Transfer the sliced green olives in the air fryer and add the tomato-meat mixture. Close the lid and cook the duck for 17 minutes.
10. Then remove the dish from the air fryer and cut the duck into the pieces. Ladle it with the tomato sauce.
11. Serve it.

Garlic duck with the pineapple honey sauce

This recipe of the duck is very easy. The main taste of the chicken is in the sliced shallot

Prep time: 15 minutes
Cooking time: 18 minutes
Servings: 4

Ingredients:
- 2 tablespoon minced garlic
- 2 duck breasts
- 1tablespoon honey
- 1 tablespoon soy sauce
- 1 teaspoon ground black pepper
- ½ cup pineapple juice
- ¼ cup fresh pineapple
- 1 teaspoon salt
- 1 teaspoon turmeric
- 1 teaspoon onion powder
- 1/3 cup shallot

Directions:

1. Take the shallow bowl and combine the minced garlic and ground black pepper. Mix up the mass.
2. Chop the duck breast coarsely and sprinkle it with the turmeric and salt. Add minced garlic mixture and stir it very carefully.
3. After this, chop the shallot and pineapple. Combine the ingredients for the onion powder, soy sauce, honey, pineapple juice, and mix up the mass very carefully till you get homogenous mass. Then transfer the mixture to the food processor and blend it for 30 seconds.
4. Transfer the duck breasts in the air fryer and pour the pineapple sauce. Close the lid.
5. Cook the dish for 18 minutes.
6. Then remove the duck breast from the air fryer and discard them from the liquid. Chill it.
7. Serve the duck with the honey sauce that was appeared after cooking in the air fryer.

Soft duck strips with jalapeno pepper

If you like hot and spicy poultry – this recipe is especially for you! You can remove the seeds from jalapeno pepper to make the dish less spicy.

Prep time: 15 minutes
Cooking time: 15 minutes
Servings: 4

Ingredients:
- 14 oz chicken
- 1 cup tomato sauce
- 1 teaspoon hot chili pepper
- 2 jalapeno peppers
- 1 teaspoon cayenne pepper
- 1 cup chicken stock
- 1 teaspoon turmeric
- 1 teaspoon basil
- 1 teaspoon oregano
- 1 teaspoon apple cider vinegar
- ½ teaspoon ground ginger
- 1 teaspoon cinnamon
- 1 big white onion

Directions:

1. Chop the chicken roughly and sprinkle it with the ground ginger and cinnamon. Stir the mixture.
2. Then peel the onion and slice it into the thin circles.
3. Chop the hot chili pepper and jalapeno pepper. Combine the ingredients together.
4. Then add basil, oregano, apple cider vinegar, turmeric, and tomato sauce. Mix up the mass very carefully.
5. After this, transfer the chicken to the tomato mixture and stir it gently. Leave the mass for at least 5 minutes.
6. Then transfer the chicken in the air fryer and pour it with the tomato mixture.
7. Cook it for 15 minutes.
8. Then remove it from the air fryer and serve it hot.

Duck roll with chickpea

This dish is very nutritious. Serve it with the main dish or eat is as a snack

Prep time: 20 minutes
Cooking time: 20 minutes
Servings: 4

Ingredients:
- 3 duck fillets
- 1 cup chickpea
- 1 onion
- 1 carrot
- 1/3 cup sweet corn
- 1 teaspoon butter
- 1 tablespoon soy sauce
- 1 teaspoon honey
- 1 teaspoon basil
- ½ cup fresh dill
- 1 teaspoon apple cider vinegar
- 1 tablespoon paprika
- 5 garlic cloves

Directions:

1. Peel the garlic cloves, onion, and carrot.
2. Chop the vegetables into the very tiny pieces. Transfer the ingredients to the mixing bowl and add basil, honey, and paprika. Stir the mixture very carefully.
3. After this, add chickpea, sweet corn, and butter. Mix up the mass again.
4. Beta the duck fillet gently and put them into the air fryer tray.
5. Transfer the filling from the chickpea in the fillets and roll it.
6. Sprinkle the roll with the soy sauce and apple cider vinegar. Cover the roll in the baking paper.
7. Then transfer the roll in the air fryer and cook it for 20 minutes.
8. After this, remove the roll from the air fryer and discard the baking paper.
9. Slice it into the thin pieces and serve it hot.

Duck with plums and dried fruits

This Christmas recipe will be great for your winter dinners!

Prep time: 20 minutes
Cooking time: 18 minutes
Servings: 4

Ingredients:
- 2 duck breasts
- 3 anise stars
- 1 teaspoon cardamom
- ¼ cup dried apricots
- 1 cup plums, pitted
- ¾ cup prunes
- 1 orange
- 1 cup chicken stock
- 1 teaspoon salt
- 1 teaspoon paprika

Directions:

1. Take the duck breast and chop them roughly. Then transfer the meat to the mixing bowl and sprinkle it with salt, paprika, and cardamom. Add anise stars and mix the mass up.
2. Chop the apricots, plums, and prunes.
3. Then cut the orange into two parts and slice it.
4. Add the fruits in the mixing bowl with the meat and stir the mass very carefully.
5. Transfer the mixture to the air fryer basket and add chicken stock.
6. Close the lid and cook the dish for 18 minutes.
7. When the duck is cooked – remove it from the air fryer and serve it on the serving plates with the juice from the meat.

Stuffed rosemary chicken

It will be the royal dish at your holiday. The rosemary will make the dish incredible!

Prep time: 20 minutes
Cooking time: 30 minutes
Servings: 6

Ingredients:
- 1 big chicken
- 2 cups rice, cooked
- 1 sweet pepper
- 1 red onion
- 1/3 cup fresh rosemary
- 1 teaspoon basil
- 1 cup fresh dill
- 1 teaspoon chili pepper
- 1 teaspoon tomato sauce
- 2 cup cream
- 1 teaspoon salt
- 1 tablespoon ground ginger

Directions:

1. Take the chicken and wash it carefully.
2. Then rub the meat with the ground ginger, chili pepper, basil, and salt. Leave it.
3. Take the mixing bowl and transfer rice.
4. Peel the onion and remove the seeds from the sweet pepper. Chop the vegetables and add them in the rice.
5. After this, chop dill and rosemary.
6. Add the chopped dill and S of all rosemary in the rice and stir the mixture carefully. After this, add tomato sauce and stir it carefully again.
7. Fill the chicken with the rice mixture. Transfer the chicken to the air fryer basket and pour the cream. Close the lid.
8. Cook the dish for 30 minutes. Then remove the chicken from the air fryer and pour it with the juice from the air fryer.
9. Let it cool little and serve it immediately.

Chicken in batter

The chicken serves the best with the grilled vegetables.

Prep time: 10 minutes
Cooking time: 20 minutes
Servings: 4

Ingredients:
- 16 oz chicken
- 1 tablespoon sriracha
- 2 eggs
- ½ cup cream
- 4 tablespoon flour
- 1 teaspoon ground black pepper
- 1 teaspoon paprika
- 1 teaspoon minced garlic

Directions:

1. Take the mixing bowl and beat the eggs with it. Whisk the mixture carefully and add cream. Stir it gently.
2. After this, add flour and stir the mixture carefully till you get homogenous.
3. Then take the chicken and transfer it to the mixing bowl. Sprinkle it with the sriracha, ground black pepper, paprika, and minced garlic. Mix the meat up.
4. Then dip the chicken in the batter and leave it for 2 minutes. Then dip the meat in the batter again.
5. Transfer the chicken to the air fryer basket and close the lid.
6. Cook it for 20 minutes or till you get a crunchy crust.
7. Then remove the dish from the air fryer and chill it little.
8. Serve it immediately.

Autumn delicious poultry stew

The great combination of the red duck meat and tender chicken will emphasize the incredible taste of the dish.

Prep time: 20 minutes
Cooking time: 20 minutes
Servings: 6

Ingredients:
- 3 sweet potatoes
- 2 red onions
- 1 duck breast
- 1 chicken breast
- 2 teaspoon red wine
- 1 teaspoon brown sugar
- 1 carrot
- 2 red sweet peppers
- 1 teaspoon chili flakes
- 1 red chili pepper
- 3 cups chicken stock
- 1 teaspoon salt

Directions:

1. Chop the chicken breast and the duck breast roughly. Sprinkle the meat with the salt and chili flakes and stir it carefully. Add wine and leave the mixture.
2. Then remove the seeds from the red sweet peppers and slice them.
3. Chop the chili pepper and combine it with the sliced pepper.
4. After this, peel the potato and onions and chop them coarsely.
5. Combine the chopped vegetables and peppers together sprinkle the mixture with the brown sugar.
6. Peel the potatoes and chop the coarsely.
7. Transfer all the vegetables in the air fryer basket and add chopped meat.
8. Pour the chicken stock in the air fryer basket and close the lid.
9. Cook the stew for 20 minutes.
10. When the stew is cooked – remove it from the air fryer and chill it briefly. Serve it.

Chicken pasta casserole

Sprinkle the hot casserole with the chopped parsley – it will make the final dish smell gorgeous.

Prep time: 15 minutes
Cooking time: 18 minutes
Servings: 6

Ingredients:
- 10 oz pasta
- 2 tomatoes
- 14 oz chicken breast, boiled
- 2 cups Parmesan
- 2 cups cream
- 1 cup green peas
- 1 teaspoon black pepper
- 1 teaspoon white pepper
- 1 tablespoon paprika
- 1 onion

Directions:

1. Peel the onion and dice it.
2. Chop the tomatoes and combine them with the diced onion. Sprinkle the mixture with the white pepper and black pepper. Stir it carefully.
3. After this, transfer the mixture to the mixing bowl and add green peas.
4. Chop the chicken breast into the medium pieces and add it to the mixing bowl too.
5. Grate the parmesan.
6. Transfer the chicken mixture in the air fryer form and add pasta. Pour the mass with the cream and sprinkle it with the grated cheese.
7. Transfer the form in the air fryer and close the lid.
8. Cook the dish for 18 minutes.
9. Then remove it from the air fryer and chill it well.
10. Serve it.

Meat

Juicy pork tenderloins

There is nothing better than juicy and tender tenderloins. Add apple cider vinegar to make the meat delightful.

Prep time: 15 minutes
Cooking time: 35 minutes
Servings: 3

Ingredients:
- 14 oz pork tenderloins
- 1 big white onion
- 1 teaspoon cayenne pepper
- 1 teaspoon oregano
- 3 teaspoon tomato sauce
- 1 cup pork stock
- 1 teaspoon salt
- 1 carrot
- 1 teaspoon soy sauce
- 1 tablespoon lemon juice

Directions:

12. Take the pork tenderloin and beat it carefully.
13. After this, take the shallow bowl and combine the salt, oregano, and cayenne pepper. Stir the mixture gently.
14. Then take the separate bowl and combine tomato sauce and pork stock in this bowl. Stir the mixture carefully till you get homogenous mass.
15. Rub the meat with the spice mixture and then pour tomato mixture in the meat.
16. Leave the mixture.
17. Meanwhile, peel the onion and carrot. Grate the carrot and dice the onion.
18. Combine the vegetables together and stir the mixture.
19. Add lemon juice and mix it up. Transfer the mixture to the meat mixture and stir it carefully again. Preheat the air fryer to 360 F and transfer the meat mixture.

Cook the dish for 35 minutes. Then remove the meat from the air fryer and discard the vegetables from the cooked meat. Serve it immediately.

Sour beef strips

This dish will be a great choice for your picnic. You can substitute honey for the maple syrup.

Prep time: 25 minutes
Cooking time: 35 minutes
Servings: 4

Ingredients:
- 20 oz beef
- 2 yellow onions
- 1 tablespoon honey
- 1 teaspoon salt
- 1 tablespoon oregano
- 1 cup celery root
- 1 tablespoon apple cider vinegar
- 1 teaspoon sriracha
- 1 cup cream
- 1 teaspoon flour
- 1 teaspoon ground black pepper
- 1 teaspoon chopped parsley

Directions:

1. Take the beef and cut it into the strips. Sprinkle the beef strips with the black pepper, salt, and sriracha. Add honey and mix the mixture up very carefully. Leave it for some time.
2. Meanwhile, peel the onion and dice them.
3. Combine the diced onions with the oregano and apple cider vinegar. Stir the mixture.
4. After this, grate the celery root and combine it with the diced onion.
5. Take the separate bowl and combine cream and flour. Stir the mixture carefully till you get smooth and homogenous mass.
6. Transfer the diced onion mixture in beef strips mixture and stir it again. Leave it for 5 minutes more.
7. Preheat the air fryer to 360 F and transfer the meat to the air fryer basket. Pour the cream mixture and stir it gently with the help of the wooden spoon.
8. Close the lid and cook the dish for 35 minutes. When the dish is cooked – remove it from the air fryer, stir it again, and sprinkle it with the chopped parsley.

Serve it immediately.

Lamb roll in bacon

The final dish is very aromatic and has a gorgeous taste. Serve the dish hot; otherwise, you will not get that special and delicious taste of the meat.

Prep time: 20 minutes
Cooking time: 35 minutes
Servings: 6

Ingredients:
- 19 oz lamb
- 13 oz bacon strips
- 2 tablespoon butter
- 1 tablespoon garlic powder
- 1 teaspoon onion powder
- 1 teaspoon Dijon mustard
- 1 cup spinach
- ½ cup chicken stock
- 1 carrot
- 1/3 cup kale
- 1 teaspoon rosemary
- 1 teaspoon thyme
- 1 tablespoon apple cider vinegar

Directions:

1. Beat the lamb meat gently and rub it with the garlic powder and the onion powder. Then add apple cider vinegar. Leave the meat.
2. After this, chop the spinach and kale. Combine the ingredients together in the mixing bowl. Add Dijon mustard and butter. Stir the mixture carefully till you get homogenous mass.
3. After this peel the carrot and grate it.
4. Add the grated carrot in the spinach mixture.
5. Take the bacon strips and sprinkle them with the rosemary and thyme. Mix up the mass.
6. Take the lamb meat and transfer the spinach mixture in the meat. Roll it.
7. Then wrap the lamb meat in the bacon strips.
8. Preheat the air fryer to 360 F and transfer the meat to the air fryer basket.
9. Pour the chicken stock. Cook the dish for 35 minutes.
10. When the dish is cooked – remove it from the air fryer and chill it for 2 minutes. Serve it.

Stuffed lamb rack

The lamb rack can have different variations. It is important to follow all the instructions to make the final dish juicy.

Prep time: 20 minutes
Cooking time: 40 minutes
Servings: 6

Ingredients:
- 26 oz lamb rack
- 1 cup millet
- 1 cup fresh parsley
- 1 teaspoon ground black pepper
- 1 teaspoon olive oil
- 1 teaspoon paprika
- 1 carrot
- 1 red onion
- 2 tomatoes
- 1 teaspoon salt
- 2 tablespoon lemon juice
- 1 tablespoon apple cider vinegar
- 1 cup beef broth

Directions:

1. Make the small cuts across the lamb rack.
2. Rub the meat with olive oil, paprika, salt, lemon juice, ground black pepper, and apple cider vinegar. Leave the meat for sometimes.
3. Peel the carrot and onion. Chop the vegetables.
4. Take the mixing bowl and combine the chopped vegetables. Add millet.
5. Chop the parsley and tomatoes. Add the ingredients in the vegetable mixture. Stir it carefully.
6. Preheat the air fryer to 355 F.
7. Fill the lamb rack with the vegetable mixture and transfer the meat in the air fryer.
8. Pour the beef broth into the air fryer too.
9. Cook the dish for 40 minutes. Then remove it from the air fryer and chill it for at least 5 minutes.
10. Serve it.

Pork roll with eggs

The roll will be softer if you combine the chicken meat and pork meat. You can use quail eggs but increase the amount of the eggs in two times.

Prep time: 20 minutes
Cooking time: 35 minutes
Servings: 5

Ingredients:
- 4 eggs, boiled
- 1 white onion
- 17 oz minced pork
- 1 teaspoon ground black pepper
- 1 teaspoon paprika
- 1 teaspoon thyme
- 1 teaspoon oregano
- ½ cup pork broth
- 1 tablespoon butter
- 1 teaspoon basil
- 1 egg

Directions:

1. Take the mixing bowl and transfer the minced pork.
2. Peel the onion and chop it Add the chopped onion in the minced meat and stir it gently. Beat the egg in the mixture and stir it carefully till you get smooth and homogenous mass.
3. After this, sprinkle the mixture with the ground black pepper, paprika, thyme, oregano, and basil. Mix up the mass carefully with the help of the hands.
4. Melt the butter and peel the boiled eggs.
5. Take the air fryer tray and transfer the meat mixture. Spread it carefully on the tray. Put the eggs on the meat and sprinkle it with the melted butter. Make the roll.
6. Preheat the air fryer to 355 F and transfer the tray with the roll. Cook the dish 35 minutes.
7. When the roll is cocked – remove it from the air fryer and chill it well. Slice it and serve it immediately.

Tender pork-beef cutlets

The main secret of the cutlets is the amount of garlic. You can add the garlic powder to emphasize the final taste

Prep time: 15 minutes
Cooking time: 30 minutes
Servings: 4

Ingredients:
- 1 cup minced beef
- 3 cups minced pork
- 1 egg
- 1 teaspoon starch
- ½ cup minced garlic
- 1 potato
- 1 teaspoon black pepper
- 1 teaspoon paprika
- 1 teaspoon cayenne pepper
- 1 teaspoon turmeric
- 1 teaspoon salt
- 1 teaspoon orange juice
- 1 teaspoon rosemary

Directions:

1. Take the mixing bowl and combine the minced pork and minced beef.
2. Take the separate shallow bowl and combine starch, black pepper, paprika, cayenne pepper, turmeric, salt, and rosemary in the bowl. Stir the mixture.
3. Peel the potato and grate it.
4. Add the grated potato to the meat mixture. Then beat the egg in the mixture too.
5. Add minced garlic and orange juice.
6. Sprinkle the meat mixture with the spice mixture and stir it carefully with the help of the hands.
7. Make the medium cutlets from the meat mixture.
8. Preheat the air fryer to 360 F and transfer the cutlets to the air fryer basket.
9. Cook the dish for 30 minutes. When the dish is cooked – remove it from the air fryer and chill the cutlets well.

   Serve the dish warm.

Aromatic beef stew

The beef is the best meat for the stew. You can combine the mixture of the asparagus and shallot to make the taste of the final dish stronger.

Prep time: 20 minutes
Cooking time: 35 minutes
Servings: 5

Ingredients:
- 1 cup red wine
- 2 red onions
- 20 oz beef
- 2 carrots
- 2 cups beef broth
- 1 teaspoon salt
- 1 teaspoon sugar
- 1 teaspoon chili flakes
- 1 tablespoon sour cream
- 3 tablespoon tomato juice
- ½ cup celery root
- 1 tablespoon oregano
- 1 cup celery stalk

Directions:

1. Take the beef and chop it roughly. After thus, transfer the chopped beef in the mixing bowl and pour it in the red wine. Stir it gently. Leave the mixture.
2. Meanwhile, peel the onions and carrot. Chop the vegetables into the medium pieces. Take the shallow bowl and combine sugar, salt, sour cream, and tomato juice together. Stir the mass carefully till you get homogenous mass.
3. After this, chop the celery root and celery stalk. Pour the tomato liquid over the meat and stir it carefully. Take the separate bowl and combine chili flakes and oregano together. Stir it.
4. Transfer the spice mixture to the meat mixture and stir it carefully again. Take the air fryer form and put the meat mixture. Add vegetable mixture and beef broth. Stir it gently. Preheat the air fryer to 360 F and transfer the stew in the air fryer.

   Cook the dish for 35 minutes. Then remove it from the air fryer, chill it little and serve it.

Stuffed onions

The onions are very tender and delicious. Serve the dish only hot. It is inappropriate to keep the stuffed onions in the fridge for some time.

Prep time: 15 minutes
Cooking time: 30 minutes
Servings: 4

Ingredients:
- 4 big white onions
- 2 cups minced pork
- 7 garlic cloves
- 7 oz Parmesan
- 1 teaspoon ground black pepper
- ¾ cup beef broth
- 1 teaspoon salt
- 1 tablespoon butter
- 1 teaspoon turmeric
- 1 teaspoon rosemary

Directions:

1. Peel the white onions and garlic cloves and cut the onions into the thick circles.
2. Grate Parmesan cheese.
3. Take the mixing bowl and combine minced pork and ground black pepper in the bowl. Add salt, turmeric, and rosemary. Stir the mixture very carefully.
4. Mince the garlic and add it to the meat mixture.
5. Take the air fryer basket and pour the beef broth. Then transfer the onion circles in the air fryer basket too.
6. Fill the onion circles with the meat mixture and sprinkle them with the grated cheese.
7. Close the lid and cook the dish at 360 F for 30 minutes. You will get the crunchy crust at the end of the cooking.
8. When the onions are cooked – remove them from the air fryer and let them cool for 5 minutes.
9. Serve the onions circles immediately.

Lamb casserole

You have never tried such a soft and delightful casserole. The dish is very nutritional so that you can serve it as the main dish for dinner.

Prep time: 15 minutes
Cooking time: 35 minutes
Servings: 4

Ingredients:
- 15 oz lamb
- 4 potatoes
- 1 zucchini
- 1 cup green beans
- 1 eggplant
- 1 cup sweet corn
- 1 cup chicken stock
- 2 cup Parmesan
- 1 teaspoon salt,
- 1 teaspoon paprika
- 1 teaspoon black pepper
- 1 teaspoon basil
- 5 oz rice noodles
- 1 cup cream

Directions:

1. Take the lamb meat and mince it. Sprinkle the meat with the black pepper, basil, and paprika. Stir the mixture carefully.
2. After this, chop the zucchini and the eggplant into medium pieces and add sweet corn and green beans.
3. Grate Parmesan cheese.
4. Combine the cream with salt and stir the mixture till salt is dissolved.
5. After this, peel the potatoes and slice them.
6. Take the big air fryer tray and pour chicken stock.
7. Then put sliced potato and chopped vegetables.
8. After this, add rice noodles and meat.
9. Sprinkle the mixture with the grated cheese. Pour the cream in the mixture too.
10. Preheat the air fryer to 360 F and transfer the casserole in the air fryer.
11. Cook the dish for 35 minutes.
12. When the casserole is cooked – let it cool briefly and serve it immediately.

Cheese pork fillets

This is a very nutritional dish that can be a great choice for your family dinner. The pineapple makes the meat taste amazing!

Prep time: 15 minutes
Cooking time: 35 minutes
Servings: 3

Ingredients:
- 17 oz pork fillet
- 8 oz Cheddar cheese
- 1 cup pineapple
- 2 red, white onions
- 1 teaspoon black pepper
- 4 tomatoes
- 1 cup chicken stock
- 3 tablespoon mayo
- 1 teaspoon tomato sauce
- 1 teaspoon basil
- 1 teaspoon turmeric
- 1 teaspoon salt

Directions:

1. Take the pork fillet and beat it carefully.
2. Sprinkle the meat with the black pepper, basil, salt, and turmeric. Leave the meat.
3. Meanwhile, chop the pineapple.
4. Peel the onions and slice them. Slice the tomatoes.
5. Take the shallow bowl and combine mayo and tomato sauce in the bowl. Stir it carefully.
6. Rub the meat with the mayo mixture.
7. Grate Cheddar cheese.
8. Take the air fryer tray and pour chicken stock.
9. Then transfer the meat fillets in the tray. Add sliced onions and tomatoes.
10. Sprinkle the mixture with the chopped pineapple.
11. Then sprinkle it with the grated cheese.
12. Preheat the air fryer to 350 F and transfer the dish in the air fryer basket.
13. Cook it for 35 minutes.
14. When the meat is cooked – remove it from the air fryer and let it cool briefly. Serve it immediately.

Tender meat wraps

This is dish the great snack for your picnic. Serve the meat only hot. You can use the grilled vegetables for the dish.

Prep time: 15 minutes
Cooking time: 18 minutes
Servings: 4

Ingredients:
- 17 oz pork fillet
- 8 oz Cheddar cheese
- 1 cup pineapple
- 2 white onions
- 1 teaspoon black pepper
- 4 tomatoes
- 1 cup chicken stock
- 3 tablespoon mayo
- 1 teaspoon tomato sauce
- 1 teaspoon basil
- 1 teaspoon turmeric
- 1 teaspoon salt

Directions:

1. Beat the pork fillet little and rub them with the black pepper and mayo.
2. Chop the pineapple and white onions.
3. Slice the tomatoes.
4. Take the shallow bowl and combine the tomato sauce, basil, turmeric, and salt together. Stir the mixture.
5. Then combine the spice mixture and the chopped pineapple and white onions together.
6. Add sliced tomatoes.
7. Grate Cheddar cheese.
8. Take the pork fillets and put the pineapple mixture in the bowl. Add grated cheese and wrap the meat.
9. Preheat the air fryer to 350 F.
10. Pour the chicken stock and add pork rolls in the air fryer.
11. Cook the dish for 15 minutes.
12. Serve the cooked meat immediately.

Korean style pork

Try this new and original recipe of the pork. You will be satisfied but the tender and sweet taste of the meat pieces.

Prep time: 10 minutes
Cooking time: 15 minutes
Servings: 3

Ingredients:
- 21 oz pork tenderloin
- 1 tablespoon sesame seeds
- 3 tablespoon soy sauce
- 1 teaspoon olive oil
- 1 tablespoon tomato sauce
- 3 medium white onions
- 1 tablespoon fresh ginger, peeled
- 1 teaspoon brown sugar
- 1 teaspoon thyme
- 1 teaspoon coriander
- 1 teaspoon oregano
- 1 teaspoon mint
- 1 tablespoon honey

Directions:

1. Chop the pork tenderloin roughly.
2. Take the mixing bowl and combine soy sauce, olive oil, tomato sauce, and brown sugar. Stir the mixture very carefully till you sugar is dissolved.
3. After this, add thyme, coriander, mint, and oregano. Stir the mixture again.
4. Peel the white onion and chop it. Chop the fresh ginger.
5. Add the ingredients in the soy sauce mixture and add honey. Stir it again.
6. Combine the honey mixture and meat mixture together and stir it carefully. Leave the mixture for at least 10 minutes.
7. Preheat the air fryer to 400 F and transfer the meat to the basket.
8. Cook the dish for 10 minutes, then stir it carefully and sprinkle it with the sesame seeds.
9. Cook the meat for 5 minutes more.
10. Serve the cooked dish hot.

Wonderful egg roll with the minced meat

You have never tried something like this before. This dish will surprise all your guests. Serve the hot roll as the main dish for dinner or cold sliced roll as the snack.

Prep time: 15 minutes
Cooking time: 20 minutes
Servings: 4

Ingredients:
- 15 oz omelet
- 2 cups minced pork
- 1 medium white onion
- 1 big carrot
- 1 teaspoon salt
- 1 teaspoon ground black pepper
- 1 teaspoon paprika
- 1/3 cup chives, for serving
- 1 large egg
- 1 teaspoon oregano
- ½ teaspoon chili flakes

Directions:

1. Combine the minced pork and egg together in the mixing bowl. Sprinkle the mixture with the salt, ground black pepper, paprika, oregano, and chili flakes. Stir the mixture carefully.
2. Peel the onion and carrot. Chop the onion and grate the carrot.
3. Combine the vegetables together.
4. Take the omelet and spread it with meat mixture.
5. Then sprinkle it with the vegetable mixture and make the roll.
6. Wrap the roll in the baking paper.
7. Preheat the air fryer to 380 F.
8. Transfer the roll in the air fryer and cook the dish for 20 minutes.
9. Then remove the cooked dish from the air fryer and chill it little.
10. Cut the roll into slices and sprinkle the dish with the chopped chives. Serve it.

Delicious pork in the currant sauce

The fresh berries make the meat taste incredible. You can substitute the fresh berries with the frozen berries but never use the currant jam for this dish!

Prep time: 20 minutes
Cooking time: 18 minutes
Servings: 4

Ingredients:
- 1 cup fresh currant
- 1 tablespoon white sugar
- 1 tablespoon honey
- 1 teaspoon white pepper
- ½ teaspoon cayenne pepper
- 25 oz pork fillet
- 1 yellow onion
- 1 teaspoon salt
- 1 teaspoon olive oil
- 1 tablespoon butter
- 2 tablespoon water

Directions:

1. Cut the pork fillet into 4 parts and sprinkle the meat with the salt, cayenne pepper, and white pepper. Stir the mixture carefully with the help of the hands. Leave the mixture.
2. Meanwhile, transfer the currant in the blender and blend it for 1 minute or till you get smooth mass.
3. Then peel the onion and chop it. Add the chopped onion in the smooth currant mixture.
4. After this, sprinkle the currant mixture with the sugar and honey. Add olive oil and white sugar. Stir the mixture carefully till sugar is dissolved.
5. Then preheat the air fryer to 380 F and toss the butter in the air fryer basket. Melt it.
6. Transfer the meat mixture in the air fryer and cook it for 5 minutes from the both sides.
7. Then add the currant mixture and cook the meat for 8 minutes.
8. When the dish is cooked – transfer it gently to the serving plates and serve it.
9. Enjoy!

Pork knuckle

It is the perfect dish for your special day. You can be sure that the pork that is cooked by this recipe can satisfy even the most demanded gourmand.

Prep time: 15 minutes
Cooking time: 30 minutes
Servings: 4

Ingredients:
- 25 oz pork knuckle
- 2 onions
- 5 garlic cloves
- 1 tablespoon paprika
- 1 teaspoon cayenne pepper
- 1 teaspoon coriander
- 1 teaspoon ground ginger
- ½ teaspoon white pepper
- ½ teaspoon ground black pepper
- ½ cup pork stock
- 1 teaspoon thyme
- 1 teaspoon orange juice
- 1 tablespoon olive oil

Directions:

1. Wash the pork knuckle carefully.
2. Peel the garlic cloves and stuff the pork knuckle with the peeled garlic.
3. Take the shallow bowl and combine paprika, cayenne pepper, coriander, ground ginger, white pepper, ground black pepper, and thyme. Stir the mixture carefully and rub the pork knuckle with it.
4. Combine the pork stock and orange juice together and mix the mixture up.
5. Then Peel the onions and blend them in the blender till you get smooth mass.
6. Sprinkle the meat with the blended onion.
7. Preheat the air fryer to 380 F.
8. Spray the air fryer with the olive oil inside and transfer the pork knuckle in the air fryer basket.
9. Cook the meat for 10 minutes from the both sides.
10. Then pour the pork stock mixture in the air fryer and cook the meat for 10 minutes more.
11. Then remove the cooked meat from the air fryer and chill it.
12. Serve the cooked dish warm.

Beef stroganoff

This recipe of the meat is very creamy. Serve the dish with noodles or mashed potato

Prep time: 15 minutes
Cooking time: 20 minutes
Servings: 5

Ingredients:
- 25 oz beef steak
- 1 cup fresh mushrooms
- 2 tablespoon sour cream
- 1 cup bone broth
- 1 teaspoon white pepper
- ½ teaspoon ground black pepper
- 1 teaspoon salt
- 1 tablespoon flour
- 3 garlic cloves
- 2 yellow onions
- 1 teaspoon tomato sauce
- ½ cup cream
- 2 tablespoon butter

Directions:

1. Chop the beef and sprinkle the meat with the white pepper, ground black pepper, and salt. Stir the mixture carefully.
2. After this, peel the onion and garlic cloves. Slice the vegetables.
3. Take the bone broth and combine it with the tomato sauce, flour, cream, and sour cream. Stir the mixture carefully till you get smooth and homogenous mass.
4. Slice the mushrooms.
5. Preheat the air fryer to 400 F and toss the butter in the air fryer basket. Add meat and cook it for 6 minutes. Stir it.
6. Then add mushrooms, sliced onion and garlic and pour the mixture with the cream liquid.
7. Cook the dish for 14 minutes more.
8. Then remove the dish from the air fryer and stir it gently again.
9. Serve it.

Meatballs with herbs

The combination of the thyme and coriander makes the meatballs very aromatic and soft.

Prep time: 10 minutes
Cooking time: 12 minutes
Servings: 4

Ingredients:
- 1 cup minced beef
- 1 cup minced chicken
- 1 teaspoon thyme
- 1 teaspoon coriander
- 5 garlic cloves
- 1 teaspoon oregano
- 1 teaspoon lemon zest
- 1 teaspoon ginger
- 1 teaspoon salt
- 4 tablespoon tomato sauce
- 1 cup chicken stock
- ½ teaspoon ground black pepper
- 1 egg

Directions:

1. Take the mixing bowl and combine the minced chicken and minced beef in the bowl.
2. Peel the garlic cloves and mince them.
3. Add the minced garlic cloves in the meat mixture. Stir it with the thyme, coriander, oregano, lemon zest, ginger, salt, and ground black pepper.
4. Stir the mixture very carefully.
5. Then beat the egg in the mixture and stir it carefully again till you get smooth and homogenous mass.
6. Preheat the air fryer to 400 F.
7. Make the meatballs from the meat mixture and transfer them in the air fryer.
8. Cook the meatballs for 2 minutes.
9. Meanwhile, combine the tomato sauce and chicken stock together. Stir the mixture till you get smooth mass.
10. Then turn the meatballs onto another side and pour the chicken stock mixture into the air fryer.
11. Cook the dish for 10 minutes more.
12. When the meatballs are cooked – remove them from the air fryer and sprinkle them with the liquid from the air fryer.
13. Serve the dish immediately.

Chili

The dish tastes great with the chili peppers. You will love the incredible aroma of the cooked chili.

Prep time: 15 minutes
Cooking time: 15 minutes
Servings: 4

Ingredients:
- 2 cups canned beans
- 1 cup minced beef
- 1 yellow onion
- ½ cup tomato sauce
- 1 teaspoon garlic powder
- ¼ cup garlic
- 1 teaspoon sugar
- ½ teaspoon cumin
- 6 oz celery
- 1 teaspoon basil
- 1 cup tomato juice
- 1 teaspoon salt
- 1 jalapeno pepper
- 1 bell pepper

Directions:

1. Take the big mixing bowl and combine canned beans and minced beef together. Stir the mixture and add tomato sauce.
2. After this, peel the garlic and slice it.
3. Chop the celery and jalapeno pepper.
4. Combine the celery, jalapeno, and garlic together.
5. Transfer the mixture to the meat mixture.
6. Add garlic powder, sugar, cumin, basil, tomato juice, and salt. Stir the mixture carefully till you get homogenous mass.
7. Slice the bell pepper and add it to the mixture too.
8. After this, preheat the air fryer to 390 F.
9. Transfer the chili mixture in the air fryer and cook it for 15 minutes.
10. Then remove the chili from the air fryer and stir it carefully. Let it cool briefly.
11. Serve the dish immediately.

Taco pie

Serve this incredible pie with the taco sauce. It is the great dish for your lunch!

Prep time: 15 minutes
Cooking time: 18 minutes
Servings: 3

Ingredients:
- 1 cup ground beef
- 15 oz Cheddar cheese
- 1 teaspoon oregano
- 1 teaspoon basil
- 1 teaspoon black pepper
- 1 teaspoon chili pepper
- 1 tomato
- 1 white onion
- 1 tablespoon minced garlic
- 1 tablespoon sour cream
- 1 teaspoon salt
- 1 teaspoon white pepper
- 10 oz puff pastry
- 1 egg yolk
- 2 tablespoon butter
- 1 teaspoon taco seasoning

Directions:

1. Take the mixing bowl and combine ground beef, oregano, basil, black pepper, chili pepper, minced garlic, and salt together. Stir the mixture carefully.
2. Peel the onion and chop it.
3. Whisk the egg yolk.
4. Take the puff pastry and roll it. Cut the dough into 2 parts.
5. Sprinkle the dough parts with the whisked egg yolk and taco seasoning.
6. Then transfer the ground beef mixture in the one part of the puff pastry.
7. Grate the cheese and sprinkle the puff pastry mass with it.
8. Add chopped onion.
9. Cover the mixture with the second part of the puff pastry and wrap the pie in the baking paper.
10. Preheat the air fryer to 400 F.
11. Transfer the pie in the air fryer and cook it for 18 minutes.
12. When the dish is cooked – remove it from the air fryer and discard the baking paper.
13. Add the sour cream and serve the pie immediately.

Cocktail meatballs

It is the best choice for your party and picnic. You can make as spicy as sweet meatballs.

Prep time: 10 minutes
Cooking time: 8 minutes
Servings: 3

Ingredients:
- 1 cup ground chicken
- 1 cup ground lamb
- 1 tablespoon minced garlic
- 1 teaspoon salt
- 1 teaspoon honey
- 1 tablespoon tomato sauce
- 1 tablespoon beef broth
- 1 teaspoon thyme
- ½ teaspoon cayenne pepper
- 1 teaspoon starch
- 1 teaspoon olive oil

Directions:

1. Take the mixing bowl and combine the ground chicken and ground lamb in the bowl. Stir the mixture and sprinkle it with the minced garlic, salt, thyme, cayenne pepper, and starch.
2. Mix the mass up till you get smooth and homogenous consistency.
3. After this, take the shallow bowl and combine honey, tomato sauce, and beef broth. Stir the mixture till all the ingredients are dissolved.
4. Preheat the air fryer to 380 F.
5. Spray the air fryer basket with the olive oil inside.
6. Make the medium meatballs from the meat mixture and transfer them in the air fryer.
7. Cook the dish for 3 minutes from the both sides.
8. After this, add honey sauce and cook the meatballs for 2 minutes more.
9. Serve the cooked meatballs immediately.

Vegetable

Veggie spice mixture

It is the best summer dish ever! It is light and nutritious. The vegetables are the great solution for your lunch!

Prep time: 10 minutes
Cooking time: 10 minutes
Servings: 4

Ingredients:
- 2 zucchini
- 2 carrots
- 1 white onion
- 1 yellow onion
- 1 tablespoon lard
- 1 cup green beans
- 1 teaspoon salt
- ½ teaspoon thyme
- ½ teaspoon basil
- 1/3 cup fresh dill
- ¼ cup vegetable stock
- 10 oz asparagus

Directions:

1. Wash the zucchini carefully and cut it into the strips. Transfer the zucchini strips in the mixing bowl.
2. Peel the carrots and onions. Chop them roughly and add the ingredients in the mixing bowl too.
3. Cut the asparagus into 2 parts and add it to the mixture too,
4. Then sprinkle the vegetables with the green beans, salt, thyme, basil, and vegetable stock.
5. Mix up the mass gently. Chop the dill and sprinkle the vegetables with it.
6. After this, preheat the air fryer to 380 F.
7. Toss the lard in the air fryer. Then add the vegetable mixture.
8. Cook the dish for 10 minutes. When the vegetables are cooked – stir them gently again.
9. Serve it immediately.

Mediterranean roasted vegetables

The sweet plums that are included in the recipe make this dish gorgeous. Serve the vegetables only hot.

Prep time: 10 minutes
Cooking time: 10 minutes
Servings: 4

Ingredients:
- 4 potatoes
- 1 cup fresh plums, pitted
- 1/3 cup cashew
- ½ cup sweet corn
- 3 bell peppers
- 1 cup cherry tomatoes
- 2 red onions
- 1 cup fresh basil
- ½ cup oregano
- 1 teaspoon salt
- 1 tablespoon olive oil
- 1 teaspoon kosher salt
- 7 oz asparagus
- 1 teaspoon apple cider vinegar
- 1 cup vegetable stock

Directions:

1. Wash the potato the carefully and do not peel the ingredients. Chop it the potato roughly and put in the mixing bowl.
2. Sprinkle it with the kosher salt and sweet corn. Slice the bell peppers and chop the asparagus roughly. Add the ingredients in the mixing bowl too.
3. Peel the onions and slice them. Chop the basil and oregano. Add all the ingredients in the mixing bowl.
4. Sprinkle the mixture with salt, olive oil, vegetable stock, and apple cider vinegar.
5. Stir the mixture carefully and add cherry tomatoes.
6. Preheat the air fryer to 400 F and transfer the vegetable mixture.
7. Cook the dish for 5 minutes. Then stir it and sprinkle it with the cashew and continue to cook the meal for 5 minutes more. When the dish is cooked – all the vegetables should be soft.
8. Serve it immediately.

Sweet potato taquitos

This dish is very friendly for children. You can add any of your favorite vegetables in the taquitos.

Prep time: 8 minutes
Cooking time: 5 minutes
Servings: 4

Ingredients:
- 4 sweet potatoes, baked
- 4 corn tortillas
- ½ cup sweet corn
- 1 cup Cheddar cheese
- 1 tablespoon tomato sauce
- 1 tablespoon butter
- 1 teaspoon oregano
- 1 teaspoon basil
- 1 tablespoon sour cream

Directions:

1. Grate the cheese and combine it with the sweet corn.
2. Combine the sour cream and tomato sauce together and stir the mixture till you get homogenous consistency.
3. Sprinkle the mashed potato with the oregano and basil. Mix up it carefully.
4. Spread the corn tortillas with the tomato sauce mixture carefully and then add mashed potato.
5. After this, sprinkle it with the grated cheese and roll the tortillas.
6. Preheat the air fryer to 400 F and put butter in the air fryer.
7. Then transfer the taquitos in the air fryer basket and cook the dish for 5 minutes.
8. Serve it immediately.

Vegetable lasagna

The lasagna can be delicious even without meat! This lasagna is very soft and creamy – the best solution for the dinner!

Prep time: 10 minutes
Cooking time: 15 minutes
Servings: 4

Ingredients:
- 4 lasagna noodles
- 1 cup spaghetti sauce
- 1 teaspoon salt
- 1 zucchini
- 1 cup fresh basil
- 1 cup cream cheese
- 1 teaspoon ground white pepper
- 1 white onion
- 1 cup mushrooms
- 1 cup cream
- 2 cups grated Cheddar cheese

Directions:

1. Peel the onions and chop them.
2. Slice the zucchini and mushrooms. Sprinkle the vegetables with the ground white pepper. Stir the mixture.
3. Combine the lasagna noodles with the spaghetti sauce.
4. Preheat the air fryer to 390 F.
5. Chop the fresh basil.
6. Take the air fryer form and put the S of the lasagna noodles in the form.
7. Then add sliced zucchini, mushrooms, and onions. Sprinkle the mixture with the chopped basil and half of the grated cheese.
8. After this, cover the mixture with the second part of the lasagna noodles.
9. Sprinkle the dish with the all grated cheese.
10. Pour it with cream and transfer the lasagna in the air fryer.
11. Cook the dish for 15 minutes.
12. Then remove it from the air fryer and chill it little.
13. Serve the lasagna warm.

Roasted garlic broccoli

The cooked dish is very soft and with the tender garlic aroma. Add the chili flakes to make the dish spicy.

Prep time: 10 minutes
Cooking time: 8 minutes
Servings: 2

Ingredients:
- 2 cups broccoli
- 1 cup garlic
- 1 teaspoon salt
- 1 cup vegetable stock
- 1 cup cream
- 1 teaspoon thyme
- 1 teaspoon cinnamon
- 1 tablespoon olive oil
- 1 teaspoon butter

Directions:

1. Wash the broccoli carefully and make the florets.
2. Sprinkle the broccoli florets with the salt and thyme. Add cinnamon and stir the mixture gently not to damage the broccoli florets.
3. Slice garlic and combine it with olive oil. Stir the mixture.
4. Add the minced garlic mixture in the broccoli and stir it carefully.
5. After this, pour cream into the mixture and leave it for 5 minutes.
6. Preheat the air fryer to 400 F.
7. Toss the butter in the air fryer. Then add broccoli mixture and roast the vegetables for 8 minutes.
8. Then remove the dish from the air fryer and chill it little.
9. Serve it warm.

Tomato cabbage stew

This stew is very nutritious and can be a great replacement of the meat dish. Add 2 types of the beans to make the taste special.

Prep time: 10 minutes
Cooking time: 20 minutes
Servings: 4

Ingredients:
- 1 cup white beans
- 15 oz cabbage
- 2 cups tomato juice
- 1 cup kale
- 1 cup chicken stock
- 1 tablespoon sour cream
- 2 sweet red peppers
- 1 cup celery stalk
- 1 teaspoon ground black pepper
- 2 cups water
- 2 white onions

Directions:

1. Chop the cabbage and combine it with the ground black pepper. Add tomato juice and stir the mixture carefully.
2. Chop the kale and celery stalk.
3. Remove the seeds from the sweet peppers and slice it.
4. Preheat the air fryer to 400 F.
5. Peel the onions and chop them.
6. Transfer the white bean in the cooking machine and pour it with water.
7. Cook it for 10 minutes.
8. Then add cabbage mixture and chopped kale and celery stalk in the air fryer too.
9. After this, sprinkle the mass with the sour cream.
10. Add sliced onion and pour chicken stock in the mixture. Stir it gently with the help of the wooden spoon.
11. Cook the dish for 10 minutes more.
12. When the stew is cooked – remove it from the air fryer and chill it little.
13. Serve the dish immediately.

Millet kale rolls

This dish can be served only hot. Add spaghetti sauce at the end of cooking to make the rolls juicer.

Prep time: 15 minutes
Cooking time: 18 minutes
Servings: 4

Ingredients:
- 10 oz kale
- 1 cup millet, cooked
- 1 cup ground chicken
- 1 teaspoon ground black pepper
- 1 white onion
- 2 bell peppers
- 1 teaspoon salt
- 1 cup tomato juice
- 1 cup vegetable stock
- 1 teaspoon basil
- 1 teaspoon oregano

Directions:

1. Chop the bell peppers and peel the onion.
2. Dice the onion.
3. Take the mixing bowl and combine the chopped bell peppers and diced onion together.
4. Add the cooked millet and ground chicken. Sprinkle the mixture with the basil and oregano. Stir it carefully.
5. Then make the leaves from the kale and fill them with the millet mixture and roll them.
6. Take the separate bowl and combine vegetable stock and tomato juice together. Stir it carefully.
7. Preheat the air fryer to 400 F and transfer the kale rolls in the air fryer basket.
8. Pour the vegetable stock mixture and cook the dish for 18 minutes.
9. Then remove the kale rolls from the air fryer and chill them well.
10. Serve the dish warm.

Cream corn

There is no something better than creamy sweet corn. It can be a great garnish for your main dish.

Prep time: 15 minutes
Cooking time: 10 minutes
Servings: 4

Ingredients:
- 18 oz corn, frozen
- 1 cup cream
- 1 cup milk
- 1 teaspoon brown sugar
- 1 teaspoon cinnamon
- 1/3 teaspoon coriander
- 3 tablespoon chives, chopped
- 1 teaspoon oregano
- 1 teaspoon turmeric

Directions:

1. Take the mixing bowl and combine cream and milk together. Sprinkle the mixture with turmeric, oregano, and coriander. Stir it carefully.
2. Preheat the air fryer to 400 F and pour the liquid mixture into the basket.
3. Cook the mixture for 3 minutes.
4. Then add sweet corn, brown sugar, and cinnamon. Stir it little and cook it for 7 minutes more.
5. Then remove the sweet corn from the air fryer and chill it little.
6. Serve it in the bowls and enjoy!

Ratatouille

Try this gorgeous dish. The great combination of the basil and Feta cheese makes the dish taste unforgettable.

Prep time: 15 minutes
Cooking time: 15 minutes
Servings: 4

Ingredients:
- 12 oz Feta cheese
- 4 tomatoes
- 2 zucchini
- 2 eggplants
- 1 cup fresh green basil
- 1 cup vegetable stock
- 3 tablespoon tomato sauce
- 1 teaspoon salt
- ½ teaspoon cayenne pepper
- 3 red onions
- 1 white onion
- 1 teaspoon olive oil

Directions:

1. Slice Feta cheese and sprinkle it with the cayenne pepper. Then wash the zucchini and eggplants carefully and slice them. Peel the white and red onions and slice them too.
2. Slice the tomatoes. Sprinkle all the vegetables with the salt.
3. Chop the green basil. Preheat the air fryer to 370 F. Take the air fryer basket and spray it with the olive oil inside. Transfer all the ingredients in the air fryer basket "one-by-one" as you see in the picture.
4. Then combine the tomato sauce and vegetable stock together and stir the mixture carefully till you get smooth mass. Pour the mixture into the air fryer basket too.
5. Sprinkle the mass with the chopped basil and cook it for 15 minutes.
6. Then let the dish cool briefly and serve it immediately.

Candied carrot

It is great garnish almost for all types of the main dishes. Add the teaspoon of the ground ginger to enforce the final taste.

Prep time: 10 minutes
Cooking time: 8 minutes
Servings: 6

Ingredients:
- 5 medium carrots
- 2 tablespoon honey
- 1 teaspoon cinnamon
- 1 teaspoon thyme
- 1 teaspoon cardamom
- ½ teaspoon chili flakes
- 2 tablespoon brown sugar
- 4 tablespoon water

Directions:

1. Peel the carrot and cut them into the medium strips.
2. Take the shallow bowl and combine cinnamon, thyme, cardamom, and chili flakes together. Stir the mixture gently.
3. After this, sprinkle the carrot strips with the brown sugar and water. Stir the mixture carefully and let the carrot gives juice.
4. Preheat the air fryer to 370 F.
5. Sprinkle the carrot mixture with the spices and stir it carefully.
6. Transfer the carrot mixture in the air fryer and cook it for 7 minutes.
7. Then add honey and stir the dish gently with the help of the wooden spoon.
8. Continue to cook the dish for 1 minute more.
9. Remove the dish from the air fryer and let it cool briefly.
10. Serve it.

Cheddar cheese baked cauliflower

You can substitute your lunch with this dish. The meal is very nutritious and soft.

Prep time: 10 minutes
Cooking time: 12 minutes
Servings: 3

Ingredients:
- 15 oz cauliflower
- 1 cup cream
- 1 cup whole milk
- 2 cup Cheddar cheese
- 1 teaspoon salt
- 2 tablespoon butter
- ½ cup fresh dill
- 2 eggs
- 1 teaspoon oregano
- 1 teaspoon turmeric

Directions:

1. Take the mixing bowl and beat the eggs with it. Whisk the egg mixture very carefully.
2. After this, add whole milk and cream. Stir the mixture.
3. Wash the cauliflower very carefully and make the florets.
4. Chop the dill and combine it with the cauliflower florets.
5. After this, sprinkle the vegetables with the turmeric, oregano, and salt. Stir the mixture again.
6. Chop the butter and add it to the vegetable mixture.
7. Preheat the air fryer to 390 F and transfer the cauliflower mass.
8. Pour the cream mixture and cook the dish for 12 minutes.
9. Then remove the roasted cauliflower from the air fryer and chill it for 3 minutes.
10. Serve it immediately.

Tomalito

This type of the Tomalito will amaze you. The taste is very delightful and tender.

Prep time: 15 minutes
Cooking time: 12 minutes
Servings: 4

Ingredients:
- 3 tablespoon butter
- 1/3 cup masa harina flour
- 4 tablespoon brown sugar
- 1 cup corn kernels
- 6 tablespoon cornmeal
- 1 tablespoon milk
- 1 teaspoon salt
- ½ teaspoon ground black pepper
- 2 teaspoon olive oil

Directions:

1. Take the mixing bowl and combine masa harina, brown sugar, cornmeal, and milk together.
2. Add corn kernels and blend the mixture with the help of the blender.
3. Then sprinkle the mixture with salt, ground black pepper. Add butter and mix the mixture up till you get a smooth consistency.
4. Preheat the air fryer to 400 F.
5. Spray the air fryer basket with the olive oil inside and transfer the blended mixture.
6. Cook the dish for 12 minutes. You should get the baked surface.
7. Then remove the Tomalito from the air fryer and chill it well.
8. Serve it.

Eggplant's balls

The vegetable balls taste as the meatballs and even better. You can add grated carrot to the mixture before cooking it.

Prep time: 10 minutes
Cooking time: 8 minutes
Servings: 6

Ingredients:
- 3 eggplants
- 1 big white onion
- ½ cup bread crumbs
- 1 egg
- 1 tablespoon sour cream
- ½ teaspoon white pepper
- 7 oz Parmesan cheese, grated
- 1 teaspoon minced garlic
- 1/3 teaspoon ground ginger

Directions:

1. Wash the eggplants carefully and peel them.
2. Peel the onion.
3. Chop the eggplants and onion roughly and transfer them to the blender.
4. Blend the mixture until smooth. Remove it from the air fryer.
5. Then sprinkle the mixture with the white pepper, ground ginger, and minced garlic. Stir the mixture gently and beat the egg in the mass.
6. Stir the mass carefully till you get homogenous consistency.
7. After this, add grated Parmesan cheese and sour cream. Stir it carefully.
8. Preheat the air fryer to 400 F.
9. Make the balls from the eggplant mixture and dip them in the breadcrumbs. Transfer them in the air fryer.
10. Cook the dish for 4 minutes from the both sides.
11. When the eggplant balls are cooked – remove them from the air fryer and chill them. Serve the dish.

Delicious spinach-mushroom stew

This stew is very light and can be great lunch or snack for you. Serve the dish warm or preheated.

Prep time: 10 minutes
Cooking time: 15 minutes
Servings: 2

Ingredients:
- 1 cup mushrooms
- 2 cups fresh spinach
- ½ cup whole milk
- 1 cup cream
- 1 teaspoon salt
- ½ teaspoon ground black pepper
- 1 teaspoon oregano
- 1 teaspoon paprika
- 2 tablespoon butter
- 1 teaspoon olive oil
- ¼ cup celery root

Directions:

1. Wash the mushroom carefully and slice them. Sprinkle the sliced mushrooms with the salt and ground black pepper. Stir the mixture.
2. Then chop the spinach and combine it with paprika, oregano, and olive oil. Mix the mixture up.
3. Peel the celery root and grate it.
4. After this, preheat the air fryer to 380 F.
5. Toss the butter in the air fryer and add sliced mushrooms. Cook them for 8 minutes and then stir the mixture gently.
6. Add spinach and grated celery root. Pour the milk and cream and stir the mass gently.
7. Cook the dish for 7 minutes more.
8. Then remove the stew from the air fryer and stir it carefully again.
9. Serve it immediately.

Spinach pie

This is an excellent dish for your picnic with the family. The pie is very nutritious.

Prep time: 20 minutes
Cooking time: 30 minutes
Servings: 6

Ingredients:
- 1 teaspoon fresh yeast
- 1 cup whey
- 2 cups whole grain flour
- 1 teaspoon sugar
- ½ teaspoon salt
- 6 eggs
- 2 cups spinach
- 1 teaspoon basil
- 1 teaspoon turmeric
- 3 tablespoon butter
- 1 tablespoon cream

Directions:

1. Take the mixing bowl and combine fresh yeast and whey together. Add sugar and stir the mixture carefully till all the ingredients are dissolved.
2. Then add flour and salt. Knead the dough.
3. Chop the spinach and combine it with butter and cream.
4. Sprinkle the mixture with turmeric and basil. Stir it carefully.
5. Take the air fryer form and transfer the dough in the air fryer. Make the shape of pie in the form.
6. Then transfer the spinach mixture in the form and beat the eggs.
7. Preheat the air fryer to 390 F and transfer the pie.
8. Cook the dish for 30 minutes.
9. Then remove the dish from the air fryer and chill it well.
10. Cut the pie into pieces and serve it.

Vegan pizza

It is a good variant for your lunch. Slice the pizza and preheat it before serving.

Prep time: 10 minutes
Cooking time: 25 minutes
Servings: 6

Ingredients:
- 10 oz yeast dough
- 1 cup mashed potato
- 1 tablespoon tomato sauce
- 1 tablespoon mayo
- 1 teaspoon black pepper
- 2 white onions
- 8 cherry tomatoes
- 1 tablespoon chives, chopped
- 1 teaspoon cream
- 1 jalapeno pepper
- 1 egg yolk
- 1 teaspoon olive oil

Directions:

1. Roll the dough into the shape of a pizza.
2. Take the mixing bowl and combine the tomato sauce and mayo together. Stir the mixture carefully.
3. After this, spread the pizza dough with the sauce mixture. Add mashed potato.
4. Slice the tomatoes. Peel the onions and slice them too.
5. Chop the jalapeno pepper. Take the mixing bowl and combine the sliced vegetables together. Add chopped jalapeno and stir the mixture gently.
6. Then transfer the vegetable mixture onto the pizza dough.
7. Whisk the egg yolk and spread the pizza sides with it.
8. Preheat the air fryer to 390 F and spray the air fryer form with the olive oil.
9. Transfer the pizza in the air fryer and cook it for 25 minutes.
10. When the pizza is cooked – remove it from the air fryer and serve it hot.

Lentil' s stew

The combination of the lentils and tomatoes make the stew juicy. The final dish has sour-sweet notes.

Prep time: 15 minutes
Cooking time: 15 minutes
Servings: 4

Ingredients:
- 1 ½ cup lentils
- 4 medium tomatoes
- 4 garlic cloves
- ½ cup chives
- 1 tablespoon chicken stock
- 2 cups vegetable stock
- 1 cup green beans
- 1 teaspoon salt
- 1 teaspoon coriander
- 1 teaspoon harissa

Directions:

1. Peel the garlic cloves and slice them.
2. Chop the chives.
3. Preheat the air fryer to 400 F.
4. Pour the vegetable stock and chicken stock in the air fryer basket.
5. Add lentils and cook the dish for 10 minutes.
6. Meanwhile, combine the green beans, salt, coriander, and harissa together.
7. Add sliced garlic cloves.
8. Chop the tomatoes and add them to the mixture and stir it.
9. Add the mixture in the air fryer and stir it gently.
10. Cook the dish for 5 minutes more.
11. Then remove the dish from the air fryer and discard the liquid from the dish.
12. Serve it immediately.

Hasselback sweet potato

This nutritious dish will be appropriated for you if you follow the healthy way of life.

Prep time: 10 minutes
Cooking time: 7 minutes
Servings: 4

Ingredients:
- 4 sweet potatoes
- 1 tablespoon walnuts
- 1 tablespoon parsley
- 2 oz olive oil
- 1 teaspoon butter
- 4 garlic cloves
- 1/3 teaspoon onion powder
- 2 tablespoon water
- 4 bacon strips

Directions:

1. Wash the sweet potatoes and make the cut in them as you see on the picture.
2. Put the 1 bacon strip in every sweet potato.
3. Crush the nuts and chop the parsley.
4. Peel the garlic and chop it.
5. Add the butter to the sweet potatoes.
6. Preheat the air fryer to 380 F and transfer the sweet potatoes. Cook them for 5 minutes.
7. Then sprinkle the potatoes with the olive oil, add water and sprinkle them with the chopped parsley, garlic, crushed nuts, and onion powder.
8. Cook the dish for 2 minutes more.
9. Then remove the cooked sweet potatoes from the air fryer and chill them for 1 minute.
10. Serve the dish immediately.

Squash with apple

The meal is sweet and delicious. You can add the additional amount of the stevia extract if desired.

Prep time: 15 minutes
Cooking time: 10 minutes
Servings: 4

Ingredients:
- 2 cups butter squash
- 4 apples
- 1 cup water
- 4 tablespoon sugar
- 1 teaspoon cinnamon
- ½ teaspoon vanilla sugar
- 1 teaspoon lemon zest

Directions:

1. Chop the butter squash into the tiny pieces. Sprinkle the squash with the sugar and cinnamon. Stir the mixture.
2. After this, peel the apples and chop them into the same pieces as the squash.
3. Combine all the ingredients together and sprinkle them with the lemon zest and vanilla sugar. Add water and stir the mixture carefully.
4. Preheat the air fryer to 390 F.
5. Transfer the apple mixture in the air fryer and cook the mixture for 10 minutes.
6. Then remove it from the air fryer and stir it carefully.
7. Chill it till you get the warm mixture and serve it.
8. Enjoy!

Sweet-sour bok choy

The main secret if the dish is that it should not be soft. Add the soy sauce at the end of cooking to make the original taste.

Prep time: 10 minutes
Cooking time: 8 minutes
Servings: 4

Ingredients:
- 15 oz bok choy
- 1 tablespoons black sesame seeds
- 1 tablespoon olive oil
- 1 teaspoon kimchi
- 2 tablespoon lime juice
- ½ teaspoon white sesame seeds
- 1 tablespoon honey
- 4 tablespoon water

Directions:

1. Take the mixing bowl and combine the honey and kimchi. Stir the mixture carefully and add olive oil and water.
2. Wash the bok choy and chop it roughly.
3. Sprinkle it with the lime juice, black sesame seeds, and white sesame seeds.
4. Mix the mixture up.
5. Then preheat the air fryer to 370 F and transfer the bok choy.
6. Cook it for 2 minutes and add honey mixture. Stir it gently and cook it for 5 minutes.
7. When the dish is cooked – remove it from the air fryer carefully and chill it well.
8. Serve it immediately.

Desserts

Sponge cake

The sponge is very fluffy. The sour cherry jam makes the taste gorgeous!

Prep time: 20 minutes
Cooking time: 25 minutes
Servings: 4

Ingredients:
- 4 egg white
- 4 egg yolk
- 1 cup flour
- 1 cup sugar
- 1 teaspoon caster sugar
- 2 tablespoon brown sugar
- 1 teaspoon vanilla sugar
- 1 cup cherry jam
- 1 teaspoon butter
- 1 cup cream

Directions:

1. Take the big mixing bowl and transfer the egg whites to the bowl. Start to whisk the egg whites.
2. When you get strong peaks – add the cup of the sugar and continue to whisk the mixture till you get a smooth consistency. Then whisk the egg yolks and add them to the egg white mixture. Stir it gently.
3. Sift the flour into the egg mixture and stir it carefully.
4. Take the air fryer form and spread it with the butter. Transfer the egg mixture in the air fryer form. Preheat the air fryer to 380 F. Transfer the sponge cake in the air fryer and cook it for 25 minutes.
5. Meanwhile, combine the cream with the brown sugar and mix up the mass till you get a fluffy mixture. After this, add vanilla sugar and stir it carefully.
6. When the sponge cake is cooked – remove it from the air fryer and chill it little.
7. Cut the cake into 2 parts across. Spread the one part of the cake with the cherry jam and then add cream.
8. Cover the sponge cake part with the second part and sprinkle it with the caster sugar. Serve the cake.

Chocolate soufflé

This soufflé is so soft and will melt in your mouth. It is the best chocolate dessert you have ever tried.

Prep time: 15 minutes
Cooking time: 15 minutes
Servings: 4

Ingredients:
- 1 cup flour
- 4 tablespoon cocoa
- 1 cup dark chocolate
- 2 eggs
- ½ cup sugar
- 1 teaspoon vanilla sugar
- 1 teaspoon cinnamon
- ½ teaspoon cardamom
- 1 egg white
- ½ cup cream

Directions:

1. Sift the flour in the mixing bowl and mix it with the cocoa, sugar, and cardamom. Stir it gently.
2. Combine the eggs and egg white together in the mixing bowl and whisk the mixture with the help of the whisker.
3. After this, add cream and stir it very carefully.
4. Combine the flour mixture and the egg mixture together and stir it carefully till you get smooth and homogenous mass.
5. Then chop the dark chocolate.
6. Preheat the air fryer to 400 F.
7. Take the small soufflй forms and fill the S of every form with the dough.
8. Add chopped chocolate and add 2 tablespoons of the dough again.
9. Make these steps with all forms.
10. Transfer the soufflй in the air fryer and cook it for 15 minutes.
11. Then remove the dish from the air fryer and chill it for at least 5 minutes. Sprinkle them with the cinnamon.
12. You can serve the dish as hot as warm.

Almond cookies

It is the best tea cookies! They are easy to cook and so delicious. Be sure; your guests will love it!

Prep time: 15 minutes
Cooking time: 10 minutes
Servings: 6

Ingredients:
- 1 cup almond flour
- 1 cup wheat flour
- 1 teaspoon baking soda
- ½ cup butter
- ¼ cup milk
- ½ cup almonds
- 1 teaspoon vanilla sugar
- 1 teaspoon stevia extract

Directions:

1. Take the mixing bowl and combine the almond flour and wheat flour. Add baking soda and vanilla sugar. Stir the mixture carefully.
2. After this, add butter, stevia extract, and milk.
3. Take the mixer and mix the mixture carefully till you get homogenous mass.
4. Preheat the air fryer to 380 F.
5. Roll the dough with the help of the rolling pin and make the small circles from the dough.
6. Add the one almond nut in every dough circle.
7. Transfer the cooked into the air fryer and cook them for 15 minutes.
8. Then remove the cookies from the air fryer and chill them well.
9. Serve the cookies immediately.

Delicious blueberry muffins

The muffins taste great as warm as cold. It will be a great snack during the day.

Prep time: 15 minutes
Cooking time: 10 minutes
Servings: 4

Ingredients:
- 1 cup blueberries
- 1 teaspoon baking soda
- 1 cup flour
- 1egg
- ½ cup sour cream
- 1 teaspoon vanilla sugar
- 8 oz sugar

Directions:

1. Take the mixing bowl and beat the egg in the bowl. Whisk it.
2. Add sugar and continue to whisk the mixture for 1 minute.
3. After this, add flour and sour cream. Sprinkle the mixture with the vanilla sugar and baking soda.
4. Take the hand mixer and mix the mixture till you get smooth mass.
5. Then add blueberries and stir the dough with the help of the wooden spoon.
6. Preheat the air fryer to 390 F.
7. Fill the S of every muffin forms with the dough and transfer them in the air fryer.
8. Cook the muffins for 10 minutes.
9. When the muffins are cooked – remove them from the air fryer and chill them well.
10. Serve the dish.

Cinnamon apple pie

The great combination of the apples and pomegranate makes the pie fantastic.

Prep time: 15 minutes
Cooking time: 25 minutes
Servings: 4

Ingredients:
- 1 cup butter
- 4 sweet apples
- 1 cup pomegranate
- 1 cup flour
- ½ cup sugar
- 1 teaspoon vanilla sugar
- 1 teaspoon olive oil
- 1 tablespoon cinnamon
- ½ cup brown sugar

Directions:

1. Take the mixing bowl and combine sugar and flour. Stir the mixture gently.
2. Then add vanilla sugar and butter and mix the mixture with the help of the hand mixer till you get smooth mass.
3. Transfer the dough to the freezer for at least 5 minutes.
4. Meanwhile, peel the apples and chop them.
5. Combine the chopped apples and cinnamon together and stir the mixture.
6. Take the air fryer form and spray it with the olive oil inside.
7. Preheat the air fryer to 390 F.
8. Remove the dough from the freezer and grate it.
9. Transfer the S of the dough in the air fryer form.
10. Then sprinkle it with the pomegranate and add chopped apple mixture.
11. Sprinkle the mixture with the brown sugar and add the grated dough again.
12. Transfer it in the air fryer and cook it for 25 minutes.
13. Then remove the pie from the air fryer and chill it well.
14. Serve it.

Air fryer doughnuts

The doughnuts can be a great snack for you during the day.

Prep time: 15 minutes
Cooking time: 10 minutes
Servings: 4

Ingredients:
- 1 cup flour
- 1 cup sugar
- 1 egg
- 1 teaspoon baking powder
- 1 teaspoon vanilla sugar
- 2 tablespoon butter
- ½ cup milk

Directions:

1. Combine the flour and sugar together in the mixing bowl. Add vanilla sugar and baking powder. Stir it.
2. Add milk and butter. Then beat egg in the mixture.
3. Take the hand mixer and mix the mixture very carefully till you get smooth and homogenous mass.
4. Make the doughnuts from the dough.
5. Preheat the air fryer to 400 F and transfer the doughnuts in the air fryer basket.
6. Cook the dish for 10 minutes.
7. Then remove the cooked doughnuts from the air fryer and chill them well.
8. Serve it immediately.

Pumpkin pie

Use the sweet type of the pumpkin for the pie. In this case, you can reduce the amount of the sugar in the final dish.

Prep time: 15 minutes
Cooking time: 25 minutes
Servings: 4

Ingredients:
- 1 cup flour
- 1 cup butter
- ½ cup sugar
- 2 cups pumpkin
- 1 teaspoon cinnamon
- 2 tablespoon starch
- 2 tablespoon whole grain flour
- 1 teaspoon cardamom
- 1 teaspoon sour cream

Directions:

1. Take the mixing bowl and combine flour and sugar. Add butter and knead the dough.
2. After this, grate the pumpkin and combine it with the whole grain flour and starch.
3. Sprinkle the mixture with sour cream, cardamom, and cinnamon.
4. Transfer the mixture to the blender and blend it well.
5. Then take the air fryer form and transfer the dough.
6. Add the pumpkin mixture.
7. Preheat the air fryer to 400 F and transfer the pie to the air fryer basket.
8. Cook it for 25 minutes.
9. When the pie is cooked – remove the dish from the air fryer and chill it well.
10. Cut the pie into the slices and serve it immediately.

Sweet cheese balls

The dish will be a great addition to your lunch or as a snack for your picnic outside. Serve the balls warm.

Prep time: 15 minutes
Cooking time: 10 minutes
Servings: 4

Ingredients:
- 1 cup Parmesan cheese
- 2 eggs
- ½ cup milk
- 1 cup granola
- ½ cup caster sugar
- 1 tablespoon butter
- 2 tablespoon flour

Directions:

1. Grate Parmesan cheese.
2. Take the mixing bowl and beat the eggs in the bowl. Add milk and whisk the mixture carefully till you get smooth mass.
3. After this, add butter and flour.
4. Take the hand mixer and mix the mixture for 2 minutes.
5. Add sugar and grated Parmesan. Stir the mixture.
6. Then make the medium balls from the cheese mixture and dip the balls in the granola.
7. Preheat the air fryer to 380 F and transfer the cheese balls in the air fryer.
8. Cook the dish for 10 minutes.
9. Then remove the cooked cheese balls from the air fryer and chill them well.
10. Serve the dish immediately or keep it in the fridge.

Cottage cheese and carrot parts

Take the fat cottage cheese for the dish; otherwise, you will not get the homogenous structure of the cooked meal.

Prep time: 15 minutes
Cooking time: 25 minutes
Servings: 6

Ingredients:

- 2 cups cottage cheese
- 1 large carrot
- 5 eggs
- 1 cup sugar
- 1 teaspoon vanilla sugar
- 1 teaspoon cardamom
- 2 teaspoon sour cream
- 4 tablespoon butter

Directions:

1. Peel the carrot and grate it.
2. Transfer the cottage cheese to the blender and blend the ingredient for 1 minute.
3. Then add eggs and sugar. Continue to blend the mixture for 2 minutes.
4. Then remove the mixture from the blender and sprinkle it with the vanilla sugar and cardamom.
5. After this, add butter and sour cream. Stir the mixture carefully.
6. Add grated carrot and stir it again.
7. Preheat the air fryer to 390 F.
8. Transfer the cottage cheese mixture in the air fryer and cook it for 25 minutes.
9. When the dish is cooked – remove it from the air fryer and chill it well.
10. Cut it into the parts and serve it immediately.

Banana puffs

This dish should be served hot or preheated.

Prep time: 15 minutes
Cooking time: 10 minutes
Servings: 4

Ingredients:
- 12 oz puff pastry
- 3 bananas
- 1 egg yolk
- 1 tablespoon water
- 1 teaspoon olive oil
- 1 tablespoon brown sugar
- 1 teaspoon lemon juice

Directions:

1. Take the puff pastry and roll it with the help of the rolling pin.
2. Then peel the bananas and blend them in the blender till you get smooth mass.
3. Then remove the bananas from the blender and sprinkle them with the lemon juice and brown sugar. Stir the mixture.
4. Whisk the egg yolk and combine it with the water. Stir it carefully.
5. Make the squares from the puff pastry and fill them with the banana mixture. Make the puffs.
6. Then preheat the air fryer to 390 F.
7. Sprinkle the puffs with the egg yolk mixture and transfer them in the air fryer.
8. Cook them for 10 minutes.
9. Then remove the cooked dish from the air fryer and chill it for at least 3 minutes.
10. Serve it.

Fried bananas

This is the kid-friendly dish. It is very fast to cook but very delicious. Your kids will love it.

Prep time: 10 minutes
Cooking time: 5 minutes
Servings: 4

Ingredients:
- 1 cup bread crumbs
- 4 bananas
- 2 tablespoon corn flour
- 2 eggs
- 1 tablespoon sugar
- 1 teaspoon cinnamon

Directions:

1. Peel the bananas and cut them into two parts.
2. Beat the eggs in the mixing bowl and whisk them carefully.
3. Then add sugar, cinnamon, and corn flour and stir the mixture carefully till you get smooth mass.
4. Dip the bananas in the liquid mixture.
5. Then dip the fruits in the bread crumbs.
6. Preheat the air fryer to 400 F and transfer the bananas.
7. Cook the dish for 5 minutes.
8. Then remove the fruits from the air fryer and chill it well.
9. Serve it.

Cinnabons

You can serve the cinnabons with the icing or without. You can add any of your favorite spices in the dish.

Prep time: 20 minutes
Cooking time: 30 minutes
Servings: 6

Ingredients:
- 1 teaspoon yeast
- 2 cups flour
- ¼ cup milk
- 1 teaspoon vanilla sugar
- ½ cup brown sugar
- 3 tablespoon cinnamon
- 1 teaspoon salt
- 10 oz butter
- 1 teaspoon olive oil
- 1 egg white
- 1/3 cup caster sugar

Directions:

1. Take the mixing bowl and combine yeast and milk together. Stir the mixture carefully till the yeast is dissolved.
2. Then add 1 teaspoon of the brown sugar and stir it carefully. Sprinkle the mixture with salt.
3. Add butter and all flour. Knead the dough.
4. Then combine the vanilla sugar, all brown sugar, and cinnamon together. Stir the mixture.
5. Roll the dough with the help of the rolling pin and sprinkle it with the cinnamon mixture.
6. Roll the dough and cut it into the medium buns.
7. Leave the buns for at least 5 minutes.
8. Preheat the air fryer to 400 F.
9. Spray the air fryer basket with the olive oil inside and transfer the buns to the basket.
10. Cook the cinnabons for 30 minutes.
11. Meanwhile, whisk the egg white till you get soft peaks.
12. Add caster sugar and stir it carefully until smooth.
13. When the cinnabons are cooked – remove them from air fryer and chill them well.
14. Sprinkle the cooked cinnabons with the egg white mixture (icing) and serve it.

Baked apples

The natural sweeteners make the baked apples so aromatic and soft. Sprinkle the final dish with the vanilla sugar.

Prep time: 10 minutes
Cooking time: 7 minutes
Servings: 4

Ingredients:
- 4 sweet-sour apples
- ½ cup walnuts
- ¼ cup raisins
- 3 tablespoon honey
- 1 teaspoon cinnamon
- ½ teaspoon ground white pepper
- 1 tablespoon butter
- ¼ cup dried apricots

Directions:

1. Wash the apples carefully and remove the meat from them.
2. Chop the apple meat very carefully and combine it with the raisins.
3. Crush the walnuts and add them to the raisin mixture.
4. Then chop the dried apricots and add them to the mixture too.
5. Add raisins and butter.
6. Transfer the mixture to the blender and blend it until smooth.
7. Then add ground black pepper and cinnamon. Stir the mixture.
8. Fill the apples with the raisin mixture.
9. Preheat the air fryer to 380 F.
10. Transfer the stuffed apples in the air fryer and cook them for 7 minutes.
11. Then remove the baked apples and chill them for 2 minutes.
12. Serve the dish warm but never cold.

Peach boards

If you do not have fresh peaches – you can add the peach jam in the boards.

Prep time: 10 minutes
Cooking time: 25 minutes
Servings: 4

Ingredients:
- 4 fresh peaches
- 2 egg yolks
- 4 tablespoon sugar
- ¼ teaspoon salt
- ¼ teaspoon cinnamon
- 1 teaspoon ground cardamom
- 14 oz puff pastry
- 3 tablespoon butter

Directions:

1. Take the puff pastry and roll it with the help of the rolling pin.
2. Take the air fryer small forms and transfer the dough.
3. Then combine the butter and salt together and stir it carefully.
4. Sprinkle every puff pastry boat with the tablespoon of sugar.
5. Separate the peaches into 2 parts and slice them.
6. Transfer sliced peaches in the puff pastry boats.
7. Then sprinkle the dish with the cinnamon and ground cardamom.
8. Add butter mixture.
9. Whisk the egg yolk and sprinkle the peach boats with it.
10. Preheat the air fryer to 395 F and transfer the peach boats in the air fryer basket.
11. Cook the dish for 25 minutes.
12. Then remove the cooked dish from the air fryer and chill it well.
13. Serve it immediately.

Sweet lemon bread

The dish will be great for your morning tea. Serve it with the lemon Kurd.

Prep time: 20 minutes
Cooking time: 30 minutes
Servings: 6

Ingredients:
- 1 teaspoon baking soda
- 1/3 teaspoon baking powder
- 2 tablespoon lemon juice
- 1/3 cup lemon zest
- ¼ cup lemon Kurd
- 1 cup skim milk
- 4 cups flour
- 1/3 teaspoon rosemary
- 1 teaspoon olive oil
- 1 cup sugar

Directions:

1. Take the mixing bowl and sift the flour into the bowl. Add baking powder and baking soda. Sprinkle the mixture with the lemon juice and stir it very carefully.
2. Then combine the lemon zest and lemon Kurd together. Add skim milk and rosemary and stir the mixture very carefully. Add sugar.
3. Then combine the flour mixture and the skim milk mixture together and knead the dough.
4. Leave the dough for 10 minutes.
5. Meanwhile, preheat the air fryer to 400 F.
6. Take the air fryer form and spray it with the olive oil inside.
7. Transfer the dough in the air fryer form and cook it in the air fryer for 30 minutes.
8. Then remove the dish from the air fryer and chill it little.
9. Then discard the dish from the form and slice it.
10. Serve it.

Cherry Dumplings

Use the frozen cherries for the filling. It will help to reduce the big amount of the liquid in the final dish

Prep time: 10 minutes
Cooking time: 7 minutes
Servings: 4

Ingredients:
- 3 tablespoon cocoa powder
- 2 cups flour
- 1 teaspoon baking powder
- ½ cup whey
- 1 tablespoon sugar
- 1 tablespoon butter
- 1 cup cherry, pitted
- 1 tablespoon caster sugar
- 1 egg

Directions:

1. Combine the flour and baking powder together. Stir the mixture.
2. Then beat the egg in the separate bowl and whisk it.
3. Add sugar and stir the mixture carefully.
4. Then add whey and stir it again.
5. After this, combine the liquid mixture and flour mixture together and knead the plastic and soft dough.
6. Roll it with the help of the rolling pin and make the small circles from the dough.
7. Fill every circle with the pitted cherry and make the small balls.
8. Dip the dumplings in the cocoa powder.
9. Preheat the air fryer to 390 F and toss the butter in the air fryer basket.
10. Then transfer the dumpling balls in the air fryer and cook the dish for 7 minutes.
11. When the dumplings are cooked – remove them from the air fryer and sprinkle them with the caster sugar carefully.
12. Serve the dumplings hot.

Plum buns

Sprinkle the buns with the sesame seeds before cooking or with any of your favorite spices to enforce the final smell of the buns.

Prep time: 15 minutes
Cooking time: 30 minutes
Servings: 6

Ingredients:
- 1 tablespoon yeast
- 2 cups warm milk
- 1 teaspoon sugar
- 1/3 teaspoon salt
- ½ cup brown sugar
- 4 cups flour
- 1 cup fresh plums, pitted
- 1 teaspoon cardamom
- 1 tablespoon butter
- 1 egg yolk
- 2 tablespoon water

Directions:

1. Take the mixing bowl and combine the yeast and warm milk. Add sugar and stir the mixture carefully till the yeast is dissolved.
2. Then add salt and flour. Knead the dough. Leave it.
3. Take the egg yolk and whisk it carefully. Add water and stir the mixture.
4. Then roll the dough with the help of the rolling pin and make the small buns.
5. Stuff the buns with the pitted plums, cardamom, and brown sugar.
6. Sprinkle the buns with the egg yolk mixture.
7. After this, preheat the air fryer to 380 F.
8. Toss the butter in the air fryer and then transfer the plum buns in the air fryer. Cook the dish for 30 minutes.
9. Then remove the buns from the air fryer and chill them briefly.
10. Serve the dish immediately.

Caramel pie

Serve the pie only hot – the caramel in the dish should be hot!

Prep time: 20 minutes
Cooking time: 30 minutes
Servings: 5

Ingredients:
- 1/3 cup cocoa powder
- 1 teaspoon baking soda
- 1 tablespoon apple cider vinegar
- 2 cups flour
- 1 cup hot caramel
- 1 cup sour cream
- 1 cup sugar
- 1 teaspoon thyme
- 1 teaspoon vanilla sugar

Directions:

1. Combine the cocoa powder and baking soda together.
2. Add apple cider vinegar, flour, and sugar. Stir the mixture.
3. Add the sour cream and thyme.
4. Take the mixer and mix the mixture until smooth.
5. Sprinkle the mixture with the vanilla sugar and stir it carefully again.
6. After this, preheat the air fryer to 400 F and transfer the mixture in the air fryer.
7. Cook it for 30 minutes.
8. Then remove it from the air fryer and chill it well.
9. Cut the chocolate across and cover every part with the hot caramel.
10. Then cut the dish for serving.
11. Serve it immediately.

Cheesecake

It is the easiest way of cooking the cheesecake. If you are a freshman in the cooking, this recipe is exactly for you.

Prep time: 10 minutes
Cooking time: 15 minutes
Servings: 4

Ingredients:
- 1 cup cottage cheese
- 3 egg yolks
- 1 cup sponge cookies
- ¼ cup butter
- 1 teaspoon sugar
- ¼ cup brown sugar
- 1 teaspoon stevia
- 1 teaspoon thyme
- ½ teaspoon vanilla extract

Directions:

1. Crush the cookies carefully and combine the mixture with the butter. Add thyme and stevia. Stir it carefully till you get homogenous mass.
2. Then whisk the egg yolks with sugar and add vanilla extract.
3. Transfer the cottage cheese to the blender and add egg yolk mixture. Blend the mixture until smooth.
4. Add butter and blend it for 1 minute more.
5. Then take the air fryer form and transfer the sponge cookie mixture.
6. Add the cottage cheese mixture.
7. Preheat the air fryer to 380 F and transfer the cheesecake in the air fryer.
8. Cook the dish for 15 minutes or till you get roasted surface of the dish.
9. Then remove the cheesecake from the air fryer and chill it little.
10. After this, discard the cheesecake from the form and cut it into pieces.
11. Serve it immediately.

Oatmeal cookies

The cookies are very light and can be kept more than 6 days.

Prep time: 10 minutes
Cooking time: 25 minutes
Servings: 6

Ingredients:
- 1 cup oatmeal
- 2 cups whole grain flour
- 2 eggs
- 1 teaspoon ground black pepper
- 1/3 cup sugar
- 1 cup butter
- 2 teaspoon olive oil
- ½ teaspoon baking soda
- 1 tablespoon lemon juice
- 3 tablespoon brown sugar

Directions:

1. Take the mixing bowl and combine the oatmeal and whole grain flour together. Stir it gently.
2. Combine the baking soda and lemon juice together and stir the mixture.
3. Add the baking soda mixture in the flour mixture
4. Then add butter and beat the eggs. Sprinkle it with the ground black pepper.
5. Sprinkle the mixture with the sugar and mix it with the help if the hand mixer.
6. Knead the dough.
7. Preheat the air fryer to 380 F and spray the air fryer basket with the olive oil inside.
8. Make the round cookies from the dough and transfer them in the air fryer.
9. Cook the cookies for 25 minutes.
10. Then remove the cookies from the air fryer and chill them well. Sprinkle the cookies with the brown sugar.
11. Serve the dish immediately.

Conclusion

The air fryer is the new generation of the kitchen tools. The food that was cooked in the air fryer is very delicious. This magic tool has a lot of benefits in compare with another kitchen machines. Let's consider some of them.

One of the most important advantages of the air fryer that differ it from all another tool is a fast time of cooking the food. Cooking the meat less than in 20 minutes is possible. If we talk about vegetables – they can be cooked less than in 10 minutes. There is the big mistake when people think that it is impossible to cook the difficult types of the dishes in the air fryer. Be sure that you can cook all types of the dish – everything you need is to follow the recipe and the instructions for cooking.

Air fryer is the best kitchen tool for busy people who are not ready to spend a lot of time for preparing dinner or lunch.

The air fryer will be good for you if you follow the healthy way of life or any the diet.

One more benefit of the kitchen machine is that the dish can be cooked with the minimum adding of the oil or any other fat. It is also possible to cook the dish without oil at all – the dish during the cooking will not burn.

The basket of the air fryer is developed in the way to prevent the unwanted food smell in your kitchen.

The air fryer is very easy to clean. You do not need any special powders and gels for cleaning the machine. Everything you need is water and detergent for washing the dishes. It is important to use a sponge instead of sharp brushes during cleaning to not damage the surface of the air fryer basket.

This wonderful book contains the most delicious and useful recipes that can be appropriate for every day. You can be sure that your family will enjoy every your new dish!

Note from the author:
If you've enjoyed this book, I'd greatly appreciate if you could leave an honest review on Amazon.
Reviews are very important to us authors, and it only takes a minute to post.

Thank you